Beyond Selling
The Ultimate Guide to Sales Enablement

Verses Kindler Publication

Verses Kindler Publication.

Website: www.verseskindlerpublication.com

Beyond Selling: The Ultimate Guide to Sales Enablement

By: Mr. Aaryendr Rajpurohit

ISBN: 978-93-5605-770-8

NON-FICTION

1st Edition

Price: INR 250/ $12

Disclaimer

Beyond Selling: The Ultimate Guide to Sales Enablement is written by Aaryendr Rajpurohit.

The published work is the original contents of the author and he has done his best to edit and make it plagiarism-free.

The characters may be fictitious or based on real events but they are not meant to hurt anyone's feelings nor portray anything against any caste or system. Any resemblance of names of actual person, place or institute is purely coincidental to carry forward the story.

In case of any plagiarized write-up, the author is solely responsible for it, the publisher would not be responsible for it.

Index

Chapter 1: The Power of Sales Enablement

Sarah watched the raindrops roll slowly down the glass, listening to the gentle taps of the water hitting the window and the soft brush of the rain on the grass outside. The scene outside the window was blurred by the lines of water, but it didn't matter, she had the image ingrained in her mind from all the afternoons spent staring out the same window. With a sigh, Sarah Miller, an experienced sales representative with a keen sense of problems and an excel sheet full of cold leads, shut her laptop. The new marketing strategy, which consisted of a series of cryptic tweets promising a "sales revolution," offered little consolation as her quota loomed large over her like a thunder cloud.

A notification appeared on her screen at that moment. The subject line of an unknown email address read, "The Key to Closing Every Deal." Sarah was itching to know more. She discovered a lone, mysterious video after clicking the link. In a dimly lit warehouse, a lone stranger with shadow cast over his face was wearing a black hoodie.

"Are you having trouble reaching your target?" a garbled voice asked. "Weary of vacuous claims and antiquated strategies? The solution is here." A close-up of a shimmering silver case was shown in the video. "The closer's edge," the voice said once more. "Unleash its potential, and watch your sales soar."

Sarah was intrigued and a little dubious, so she looked further. The sender, a mysterious group going only by "The Enablers," requested for her input on the present problem statement in return for a free trial of the "A guide to enhancing sales". She felt a chill run down her spine, but she could not deny the benefit. Was this a sophisticated marketing gimmick, or was there something more?

Sarah decided to bite the bait and took a big breath. The thought of missing her quota once more was too depressing to entertain. She had no idea that this choice would take her on a fast-paced adventure into the cutting edge of sales enablement, where the distinction between manipulation and technology becomes hazy and deal-closing secrets might have lethal consequences.
***
Just like Sarah Miller, there are many sales people out there, in the modern corporate environment, which is so competitive that having a skilled sales staff is insufficient. Companies that want to succeed must provide their sales representatives with the instruments, know-how, and tactics necessary to interact with prospects, meet their needs, and eventually increase revenue. We call this ongoing, strategic approach "sales enablement."

Imagine a symphony orchestra. Each musician is skilled in their own right, but it's the conductor who brings harmony, ensuring that each instrument contributes to a beautiful, cohesive performance. Sales Enablement is the conductor in the orchestra of sales, orchestrating processes, technology, and talent to create a harmonious and high-performing sales team.

Sales enablement technologies are a key factor in productivity increase because they automate repetitive operations and streamline workflows, freeing up sales representatives to concentrate on high-impact activities that actually make a difference.

Comprehensive sales enablement programmes shorten the learning curve and make new hires effective team members more quickly, making onboarding them a breeze. Data becomes your greatest friend, and sales enablement technologies offer insightful analysis and insights to assist in pinpointing problem areas and maximize sales tactics. Representatives who have gained the knowledge and resources necessary for success feel empowered, driven, and prepared to take on any challenge, which boosts morale. Lastly, and maybe most significantly, sales enablement yields quantifiable ROI. Sales enablement programmes show their worth in practice by having a direct influence on important KPIs like revenue growth, win rates, and sales cycle duration.

Strong sales enablement strategies significantly increase win rates, shorten sales cycles, and increase overall quota achievement, according to studies from reputable organisations like CSO Insights and Gartner. However, the influence extends beyond personal achievement. Businesses who use sales enablement have an average 20% quicker rate of revenue development. It is a company-wide accelerator.

This is not where the tale of sales enablement ends. This chapter has shown you how powerful it can be, but the next one goes even farther, showing you how sales enablement techniques have come a long way from their simple origins to their complex, data-driven form today. We'll learn how the idea has evolved in tandem with consumer expectations, technological advancements, and the dynamic business environment. So grab a seat, because we are just getting started on this adventure into the realm of sales enablement.

The Impact of Sales Enablement: Real-World Success Stories

To bring the concept of Sales Enablement to life, let's explore a few real-world success stories.

Case Study 1: Company X, a leading software firm, struggled with inconsistent sales performance and long sales cycles. By implementing a robust Sales Enablement strategy, they were able to reduce the sales cycle by 30% and increase their win rate by 20%. The key was a comprehensive content library, regular training sessions, and the integration of an advanced CRM system.

Case Study 2: Company Y, a B2B manufacturing giant, faced challenges in aligning its sales and marketing teams. Through Sales Enablement, they fostered collaboration between these departments, resulting in more targeted marketing campaigns and higher-quality leads. This alignment led to a 25% increase in revenue within a year.

Components of Sales Enablement

Some of the commonly used terms in sales enablement are -

Content production and curation	Producing presentations, case studies, battle cards, and other high-quality sales materials in association with product marketing.
Coaching and training	Assist representatives in honing their abilities, offer them individualised coaching and continuous training programmes.
Adoption of technology	Choosing and putting into practice sales enablement

	solutions including content management systems, sales automation software, and CRM platforms.
Sales Process Optimization	Streamlining the sales funnel to maximise effectiveness and efficiency is known as sales process optimization.
Departmental alignment	Encouraging cooperation amongst the customer success, marketing, product and sales teams.

Advantages of Implementing Sales Enablement

The advantages of sales enablement spread like wildfire throughout your company, producing a series of favourable consequences. A more motivated and effective sales force results from empowered representatives having the appropriate resources and expertise, which boosts their confidence. Here are some of the benefits of sales enablement-

- Better sense of direction- Sales enablement data enables managers to support individual talent by offering tailored coaching and development.
- Collaborative effort- Thanks to common resources, consistent messaging, and streamlined procedures, sales, marketing, product and customer success work together harmoniously to foster collaboration.
- Rapid growth- Last but not least, because sales enablement is data-driven, you can quantify its influence on win rates, revenue growth, and customer happiness, demonstrating its worth and defending ongoing investment.

To put it briefly, sales enablement is a calculated investment that maximises revenue growth, optimises workflow, and equips your sales force for success.

Quantifying the Impact

Numerous studies highlight the positive impact of sales enablement on sales performance. According to a study by CSO Insights, companies with strong sales enablement practices experience:

- 50% higher win rates
- 33% shorter sales cycles
- 18% higher sales quota attainment

Sales enablement not only boosts individual rep performance but also impacts overall business success.

The Evolution of Sales Enablement

Early Days (Pre-1990s)

Imagine a world without computers, smartphones, or even the internet. This was the reality for salespeople in the pre-1990s era. Sales enablement in this period was a far cry from its current form. The primary focus was equipping reps with basic product knowledge. Training, often delivered in a classroom setting, centered around product features and benefits. Collateral materials like printed brochures and sales scripts served as the foundation for prospecting and sales conversations. There was little to no coaching, if any at all. Salespeople had to rely only on their charm and human qualities to close deals; there was hardly any usage of technology.

This approach may appear antiquated by today's standards, yet it was effective in a less complicated corporate environment. But the flaws in this basic paradigm became obvious as consumer expectations rose and markets got more competitive.

The Rise of Technology (1990s-2000s)

The introduction of Customer Relationship Management (CRM) systems in the 1990s marked a significant turning point for sales enablement. These systems offer a centralised platform for tracking interactions, maintaining customer data, and managing sales pipelines. Representatives suddenly had a wealth of information at their fingertips for the first time, enabling them to tailor their approach and modify their sales pitches to specific consumer demands.

In the 2000s, tools for automating sales started to appear. These cutting-edge technologies make tasks like lead generation, email marketing, and activity tracking easier. Reps were able to concentrate on developing connections and closing business because this gave them back crucial time. There has also been a change in content generation towards digital assets. Bulky printed materials were replaced with interactive presentations, online training courses, and product demos, providing sales representatives with a more accessible and interesting learning environment.

In addition, around this time the idea of data-driven decision making surfaced. Sales managers started using metrics from automation systems and CRM to monitor representative performance, pinpoint areas for development, and assess how well sales enablement initiatives were working. The increased emphasis on data analysis made sure that sales activities were focused and in line with the overarching objectives of the company.

The Era of Customer Centricity (2010s-2020s)

A paradigm shift in sales enablement was brought about by the rise of customer centricity in the 2010s. The days of aggressive sales techniques were over. Building trusting relationships with customers and learning about their particular needs became the main priorities. Training on social selling methods, content marketing approaches, and utilising social media platforms to interact with prospects and present thought leadership started to be included in sales enablement programmes.

The distinctions between traditional sales and marketing tasks have also become more hazy in the digital age. Programmes for sales enablement began to place a strong emphasis on producing material that addressed the whole purchasing process, from first awareness to final purchase decision.

The Post Covid-19 Era (2020s-Present)

The pandemic of COVID-19 provided a harsh education in sales enablement agility. Virtual meetings have supplanted in-person contacts, necessitating a transition to online sales presentations and video conferencing software. As salespeople navigated an unpredictable economic environment, the need for data-driven insights grew critical. In order to handle a geographically distributed sales force, sales enablement programmes changed by emphasising digital content production, automating processes, and giving priority to remote coaching tactics. The landscape of sales enablement has changed as a result of this forced innovation phase, with an increased focus on data analysis, flexibility, and the power of technology in the new era of virtual selling.

How Sales Enablement Drives Sales Performance and Revenue Growth?

Beyond theory, sales enablement has enormous power. It converts into tangible, quantifiable outcomes that have an immediate effect on your revenue. We'll go into detail in this section about the specific ways that sales enablement programmes increase revenue and improve sales success.

1. Sharper Skills, Higher Win Rates:

Imagine a sales representative who is well-versed in the product, has mastered efficient communication strategies, and can easily handle challenging sales objections. This is how sales enablement can change a situation. Thorough training programmes and continuous mentoring provide representatives the tools they need to establish rapport, confidently handle client demands, and successfully complete sales.

CSO Insights studies demonstrate this effect. Businesses with effective sales enablement strategies report startling 50% higher win rates. This results in closed deals increasing, happy customers, and a notable improvement in overall sales performance.

2. Shortened Sales Cycles, Faster Revenue Generation:

Opportunities are wasted with each needless day spent figuring out a complex sales procedure. By giving representatives the instruments and resources they need to effectively move prospects through each stage, sales enablement programmes shorten the sales cycle.

- Automated Tasks: Sales automation solutions take care of time-consuming duties like email follow-ups and lead nurturing, allowing representatives to concentrate on high-impact tasks like establishing rapport and qualifying leads.
- Simplified Procedures: Standardised workflows and clearly defined sales techniques provide uniformity and remove ambiguity within the sales force.
- Data-Driven Insights: By giving sales representatives access to real-time data and analytics, sales enablement solutions help them complete deals more quickly and more effectively.

Sales enablement programmes can significantly shorten the sales cycle by removing obstacles and streamlining the process. This results in quicker revenue creation, deal closings, and, eventually, more adaptable and responsive salespeople.

3. Enhanced Customer Satisfaction, Increased Retention:

In today's customer-driven business world, building enduring relationships is essential. Programmes for sales enablement equip representatives with the resources they need to offer clients a positive and consistent experience from beginning to end.

- Deeper Product Knowledge: Sales representatives that are knowledgeable about your products or services are better equipped to connect with customers, pinpoint their specific issues, and offer solutions that actually solve them.
- Effective Communication: Training courses that have a strong focus on active listening, rapport-building, and clear communication enable representatives to engage with customers on a human level, fostering trust and loyalty.
- Personalised Approach: Sales enablement pushes representatives to modify their strategy in accordance with the unique requirements and preferences of each client. Customer relationships are strengthened and a perception of value is fostered by this personalised experience.

Sales enablement programmes help to increase customer satisfaction rates as a result of these efforts. Customer retention is higher and your revenue stream is more consistent when you have happy consumers who recommend your brand to others and make repeat purchases.

4. Amplified Productivity, Freed Up Time for Selling:

Imagine a sales rep bogged down by administrative tasks and struggling to find the resources they need. This is precisely what sales enablement programs aim to eradicate.

- Technology for Efficiency: Routine processes like data entry, meeting scheduling, and report generation are automated with sales automation software. This gives sales representatives more time to concentrate on developing connections and closing agreements, which is the main goal of selling.
- Centralised Content Management: By keeping all sales content in one location, you can easily access it and save time looking up out-of-date information.
- Streamlined Processes: Representatives can operate more productively when there is less confusion and effort duplication thanks to well-designed procedures and open lines of communication.

Through task automation, resource accessibility, and process optimisation, sales enablement programmes increase the productivity of sales representatives in general. More time spent on sales-related activities, more deals in the works, and eventually more income generation result from this.

5. Data-Driven Decisions, Continuous Improvement:

The days of a salesperson depending only on intuition are long gone. Data-driven decision making is embraced by sales enablement programmes.

- Sales analytics: Sturdy analytics tools shed light on important variables like customer behaviour, win rates, and sales cycle length. Making data-driven decisions and identifying areas for development are made easier with the use of this data.
- Performance Monitoring: Sales managers may discover top performers, correct deficiencies, and put in place focused coaching programmes by monitoring sales activities and individual representative performance in real-time.
- Programme Measurement: Sales enablement programmes can prove their worth and justify additional funding by monitoring important indicators like ROI and sales effectiveness.

This data-driven approach allows for continuous improvement within the sales enablement program. By analyzing results, adapting strategies, and refining tactics based on real-world data, organizations can ensure their sales efforts remain laser-focused and consistently deliver high performance.

The Synergy Effect:

It's important to remember that the benefits of sales enablement are not siloed. They work synergistically to create a powerful ripple effect throughout your organization. Here's how:

- Enhanced Team Morale: When reps feel empowered with the right tools, knowledge, and support, their confidence soars. They are more likely to feel motivated, engaged, and excited about their roles. This positive morale translates to a more collaborative and productive sales team environment.
- Improved Coaching and Development: Data from sales enablement tools allows managers to identify individual strengths and weaknesses within their teams. This targeted data empowers them to provide personalized coaching and development opportunities, nurturing talent and propelling individual growth.
- Alignment Across Departments: A well-designed sales enablement program fosters collaboration between sales, marketing, product and customer success teams. Shared resources, consistent messaging, and streamlined processes ensure a seamless customer experience throughout the entire buying journey. This cross-functional alignment leads

to better communication, reduces friction, and ultimately drives overall business success.

- Measurable ROI: The data-driven nature of sales enablement programs allows organizations to quantify their impact on key metrics like revenue growth, win rates, and customer satisfaction. This measurable ROI demonstrates the program's value and facilitates the allocation of resources for continuous improvement.

In my opinion, sales enablement isn't just a buzzword; it's a strategic investment with a demonstrably positive impact on your bottom line. By equipping your sales force with the right tools, knowledge, and strategies, you can unlock their full potential, streamline the sales process, and achieve sustainable revenue growth.

The future of sales enablement is bright. Advancements in technology, like AI and machine learning, will continue to revolutionize the way sales teams operate. Imagine AI-powered tools that provide real-time coaching during sales calls, analyze customer behavior to predict buying patterns, and automate repetitive tasks with even greater efficiency. By embracing these advancements and continuously adapting their strategies, organizations can ensure their sales enablement programs remain at the forefront, propelling them towards continued success in the ever-evolving business landscape.

Chapter 2: Understanding Your Market Landscape

Two different worlds of business converged in the busy metropolis of Mumbai. TechNova, a rapidly growing B2B software solutions firm, was facing the challenges of enterprise sales at one extreme of the spectrum. Their CEO, Rohan, was perplexed by the complex processes corporate clients used to make decisions. He frequently got lost in a web of stakeholders, technical assessments, and never-ending negotiations.

Just a short distance away from Technova, A fashionable e-commerce startup StyleCraze was located in the centre of the city's retail centre. Anya, their CEO, had to deal with a whole different set of difficulties. Her team was fighting to stay ahead because of the unstable nature of customer preferences, the intense competition, and the always changing digital scene. What was effective yesterday may not be so today. Both Rohan and Anya were left longing for a deeper comprehension of their clients and the most effective ways to engage with them as they found themselves staring at a market landscape that appeared to change like quicksand beneath their feet.

After a lot of research, they found that the effectiveness of sales enablement programs depends on having a thorough understanding of your target market. Business-to-business (B2B) and business-to-consumer (B2C) sales are the two main categories that rule the commercial environment today. Every market has its own distinct client behaviours, purchasing processes, and difficulties. Achieving best results require customising your sales enablement plan to address these specifications.

B2B vs. B2C Sales

B2B Sales:

Envision an intricate network in which enterprises vend goods or amenities to other enterprises. Think about a busy factory producing thousands of smartphones every day. The owner of the factory must purchase raw materials like metal and glass. In order to achieve this, they purchase from a provider that specialises in raw materials rather than from a customer directly. This business-to-business (B2B) transaction between the supplier and the factory is a prime illustration of B2B trade.

Selling goods or services to other businesses as opposed to individual customers is known as business-to-business (B2B) sales. It is the foundation of many businesses, such as software development and manufacturing, where successful operations depend on one another.

This is the B2B sales domain. In this case, the customer journey is frequently drawn out and involves several organisational decision-makers. Here are a few things you should keep in mind, when entering the domain of B2B.

- Focus: Establishing trust and forming long-term relationships with important buying group stakeholders are the usual goals of B2B sales.
- Making Decisions: Purchasing decisions typically require a thorough screening procedure that includes a cost-benefit analysis, a lot of research, and permission from a number of departments, including finance, legal, and IT.
- Sales Cycle: When numerous decision-makers are involved, the B2B sales cycle can be protracted, lasting weeks or even months.
- Customer Relationships: Establishing a rapport with influential and important decision-makers within the target organisation is crucial.

B2C Sales:

Businesses sell goods or services directly to consumers via business-to-consumer (B2C) sales. When motivated by personal needs and aspirations, the purchasing process is frequently quicker and more spontaneous. Here are some things which can help you excel in B2C sales.

- Focus: B2C sales usually place an emphasis on quick conversions by emphasising aspects and advantages of the product that appeal to the intended market.
- Making Decisions: Buying decisions are typically made more quickly and emotionally, with less focus on in-depth analyses.
- Sales Cycle: Within minutes or hours of the first product discovery, purchases typically occur in the B2C sales cycle, which is typically shorter.
- client interactions: B2C sales frequently rely on a larger client base with less personal interactions, even if developing brand loyalty is crucial.

Decoding Customer Behavior

Being able to navigate the complex dance of client behaviour is essential to developing a winning sales enablement plan. Whether you're negotiating the fast-paced B2C market or the sophisticated B2B one, it's critical to adjust your strategy to the unique needs and purchasing paths of your target market. In order to provide you with the knowledge necessary to create a sales enablement programme that resonates and converts, this section goes deeper into the primary distinctions between B2B and B2C buyers.

1. Information Consumption: Hunger for Knowledge vs. Bite-Sized Insights

B2B Buyers:

Picture a product marketer painstakingly going through a library, extracting industry publications, competition analysis, and white papers. The B2B buyer is defined by their methodical approach to information intake. They need comprehensive, data-driven materials that tackle their unique business problems and show off the observable advantages of your solution. Two things that you must keep in mind when dealing with B2B buyers-

- Cravings for Content: A B2B buyer's information diet must include white papers, case studies, webinars with industry experts, ROI calculators, and thorough product comparisons. These materials offer the information, figures, and hard proof required to support their purchase choice to various organisation stakeholders.

- Developing Expertise to Build Trust: B2B purchasers are leery of hollow promises. They are looking for thought-provoking content that positions your business as a reliable resource. Blog entries, industry papers, and attendance at pertinent conferences show off your knowledge and establish you as a useful resource for resolving their challenging business issues.

B2C Consumers:

B2C consumers, on the other hand, more closely resemble harried commuters stopping for a quick coffee and a fast news clip on their smartphone. Their desire for easily consumable content and shorter attention spans are characteristics of their information intake. Make sure to keep in mind these things when dealing with B2C consumers-

- The King of Snackable Content B2C buyers prefer to gather information from online reviews, social media comparisons, user-generated content (UGC), and quick product films. These brief but insightful content pieces provide social approval and rapid insights, impacting purchase decisions.
- Emotional Connection Above Technical Specifications: Although B2C consumers may quickly scan product details, emotions frequently influence their choices. Technical specs don't resonate as profoundly as appealing graphics, compelling brand storytelling, and good testimonials.

2. The Power of Influence: Logic vs. Emotion

B2B Buyers: Logic reigns supreme in the B2B world. They meticulously evaluate cost-savings, process efficiency, and the return on investment (ROI) your solution promises.

- **Risk Aversion and Justification:** B2B purchases often involve significant financial investments and impact multiple departments within an organization. This risk aversion translates into a focus on measurable benefits. Case studies that showcase how similar companies achieved success with your product and detailed ROI calculations become powerful tools for swaying B2B buyers.

- **The Power of the Network:** Industry analyst reports and peer recommendations are important sources of information when making B2B decisions. Good word-of-mouth from reliable sources and industry endorsements give your assertions more weight and have an impact on the assessment procedure.

B2C Buyers: Although reason does play a part, strong emotions are frequently the driving force behind B2C purchases. Buying choices can be greatly influenced by a variety of factors, including social validation, product aesthetics, brand image, and the need for self-expression.

- **The Power of Brand Storytelling**: Businesses that appeal to B2C customers' emotions and values will win them over. Strong brand narrative that speaks to the aspirations and hopes of consumers is a powerful sales tool.
- **The Influence of Social Proof:** Utilising positive social proof can assist you in harnessing the power of the crowd to sway B2C purchase decisions. For example, think of all the influencers on social media platforms. They have created an imaginary world for their followers who look up to them. These influencers use their platform and the power of social media, to drive B2C sales.

3. The Buying Journey

B2B Buyers: The process of doing business with a B2B buyer is similar to running a marathon; it's a long race with numerous competitors and checkpoints.

- **Multi-Step Process:** There are multiple distinct stages involved in B2B buying journeys, such as awareness, consideration, evaluation, selection, and execution. Personalised outreach and content strategies are required for every step. For instance, thought leadership materials can stimulate initial interest in the awareness stage, while in-depth case studies become essential in the assessment stage.

- **The Strength of Bonds:** In B2B sales, it is critical to establish trusting connections with influential decision-makers within the target organisation. The purchasing committee may include representatives from operations, IT, and finance, each with their own standards for evaluation.

- **Comprehending Individual Needs:** Customising talks and presentations to each buying committee member's unique concerns and interests.

B2C Purchasers: The path of a B2C customer is more like a sprint—a hurried race to the finish line, frequently driven by impulse or the need for instant satisfaction.

- **Purchase Process Simplicity:** Business-to-consumer customers demand a smooth and intuitive purchasing process. To turn interest into a purchase, clear product

information, user-friendly websites, and safe checkout
procedures are crucial.

- **The Power of Personalisation:** B2C sales enablement
  greatly benefits from personalisation. Conversion rates can
  be greatly raised by making relevant product
  recommendations based on previous purchases, providing
  targeted discounts, and customising marketing messaging to
  each individual customer's tastes.
- **Using the Power of Urgency**: Flash sales, limited-time
  promotions, and scarcity strategies can instil a sense of
  urgency in B2C customers and influence them to make a
  purchase.

4. Building Bridges: Content Strategies for B2B and B2C

B2B Content Strategy:

When building a B2B content strategy, keep these things in mind-

- **Put Thought Leadership First**: Make your business
  known as an authority in the field by producing top-notch
  articles that specifically target the problems and concerns of
  your intended B2B audience, such as white papers, case
  studies, and blog posts.
- **Information for Every Phase of the Purchaser Journey:**
  Create a content library that addresses every phase of the
  B2B purchasing process. In addition to providing
  comprehensive materials like white papers and ROI

calculators for the assessment stage, provide content that raises awareness, such as blog articles and infographics.

- **Utilise Various Content Formats:** Provide content in a variety of forms, such as podcasts, webinars, and video presentations, to accommodate a range of learning preferences.

B2C Content Strategy:

When building a B2C content strategy, keep these things in mind-

- **Embrace Storytelling:** Create engrossing brand narratives that emotionally engage your B2C audience. Employ narrative strategies to highlight the advantages of your offering and the ways in which it can enhance their life.

- **Optimise for Mobile Consumption:** Make sure your website and content are mobile-friendly and provide a seamless user experience, as a large percentage of B2C consumer journeys take place on smartphones.

- **User-Generated Content (UGC) Integration:** Encourage social media posts showcasing your items as well as reviews and testimonials from customers. UGC influences B2C purchasing decisions by fostering social proof and trust.

You may design a sales enablement programme that appeals to your target audience by comprehending the distinctive features of B2B and B2C client behaviour. Recall that the goal is to create a harmonious ensemble of strategies rather than a strict dichotomy.

By combining the best features of both B2B and B2C strategies—content marketing, data-driven personalisation, and relationship development—you can create a comprehensive sales enablement programme that boosts conversions and promotes long-term business expansion.

It is imperative to remain aware of the constantly shifting dynamics of consumer behaviour as the business environment changes. You may succeed in today's changing market by navigating the complex dance of B2B and B2C sales by being aware of these subtleties and adapting your strategy.

Understanding The B2B and B2C World

Even if these differences exist, it's crucial to avoid simplifying things too much. Emotions can play a role in B2B transactions, and before making a choice, B2C customers might do a lot of research. When it comes to B2B and B2C sales enablement, empathy is still an essential tool. It is possible to customise your sales technique and material to your target audience's buying behaviours and motives by knowing them.

As the corporate environment changes, the distinctions between B2B and B2C are becoming less clear. Emotions and personal preferences are influencing B2B customers more and more, particularly in industries like professional services and technology. Similarly, B2C consumers frequently carry out extensive study prior to making noteworthy purchases, obfuscating the distinctions with conventional B2B purchasing practices. Because of this convergence, companies now have a rare chance to take a hybrid approach, using aspects of both B2B and B2C sales enablement methods to meet the changing needs of their clientele.

Navigating the Buying Journey: B2B vs. B2C Sales Enablement Strategies

B2B Sales Enablement Strategies:

- **Content Marketing:** Produce top-notch materials that specifically address the demands and issues of your target B2B buyers, such as ROI calculators, case studies, and white papers in association with Product Marketing.
- **Thought Leadership**: Create thought leaders in your sales force who can offer insightful commentary via webinars, blogs, and trade journals to help you position your business as an industry leader.
- **Account-Based Marketing (ABM):** Target high-value target accounts on a pre-established list and tailor your outreach and sales support materials to meet their unique requirements.
- **Sales Automation Solutions:** To manage numerous contacts within a buying group, track progress, and expedite

the intricate B2B sales cycle, use CRM platforms and sales automation solutions.

- **Sales Coaching & Training:** Give your B2B sales representatives the tools they need to successfully manage objections, negotiate intricate sales cycles, and cultivate enduring bonds with numerous decision-makers.

B2C Sales Enablement Strategies:

- **Social Media Marketing:** Use sites like Facebook, Instagram, and TikTok to interact with your target market, present your goods in interesting ways, and increase brand recognition.
- **E-commerce Optimisation**: Make sure your website is easy to use, provides a smooth purchasing experience, and has eye-catching images and compelling product descriptions.
- **User-Generated Content (UGC):** Promote social media posts that highlight your items and customer evaluations and testimonials. Emotional UGC influences purchasing decisions by fostering social proof and trust.
- **Influencer Marketing:** Collaborate with social media influencers who are relevant to your business to reach a larger audience and use their authority to market your goods.
- **Email Marketing:** Create eye-catching email campaigns that personalise the customer experience all the way through

the purchasing process, nurture leads, and advertise special deals.

Personalised product recommendations, real-time customer data, and automated processes like email follow-ups are all examples of sales enablement technology.

The Takeaway: Tailoring Your Approach for Success

By understanding the distinct characteristics of B2B and B2C markets, you can craft a sales enablement program that resonates with your target audience. Remember, the key lies in tailoring your content, training, and technology to address the specific needs and buying journeys of your customers. Whether you're navigating complex B2B sales cycles or fostering impulse purchases in the B2C world, a well-designed sales enablement program will empower your reps to close deals and drive sustainable business growth.

Looking Ahead

The business landscape is constantly evolving, and the lines between B2B and B2C are becoming increasingly blurred. B2B buyers are increasingly researching online and engaging with social media content before making purchase decisions. Similarly, B2C companies are recognizing the value of building long-term relationships with loyal customers.

This convergence presents exciting opportunities for sales enablement. By embracing the strengths of both B2B and B2C strategies – content marketing, social media engagement, and data-driven personalization – organizations can create a holistic approach that resonates with all types of customers, regardless of their buying behavior.

The future of sales enablement lies in adaptability and a focus on the customer journey. By understanding your market, tailoring your approach, and leveraging the power of technology, you can unlock the full potential of your sales force and achieve superior results in today's dynamic business environment.

Chapter 3: The Pillars of a Winning Sales Enablement Program

Sarah a youthful and driven sales representative. After graduating from university, Sarah joined a tech business that was booming, her brain full of ambitions and briefcase full of hope. 'Technova' was a corporation whose goal was to transform the business software market. But Sarah quickly learned that selling was a sophisticated dance, a high-stakes game where every move mattered, and it required more than simply charm and persuasion.

Sarah encountered a plethora of obstacles that caused her initial enthusiasm to fade. Technical details appeared to pique prospects' attention more than business results. There were numerous stakeholders requesting attention while the sales cycle continued on forever. Sarah also had the feeling of being a lone adventurer lost in an unfamiliar country without a compass in the middle of the mayhem.

At that point, Sarah was taken under the wing of her manager, Marcus, an elderly sales veteran. One important lesson Marcus imparted was this: "Selling isn't just about the product; it's about understanding the customer's world and providing solutions that resonate." Marcus then set out on a mission to provide Sarah with the resources, information, and assistance required to succeed in the cutthroat world of sales.

Sarah's path would take her through a maze of sales enablement, teaching her about the benefits of coaching, training, and content, as well as the revolutionary possibilities of technology. It was a journey that would mould Sarah's professional life and establish the groundwork for Technova's sales success. For Sarah to understand sales enablement in depth, it was necessary to understand its four fundamental pillars.

Four Fundamental Pillars

Consider a building that is rising up towards the clouds. A strong foundation is necessary for its strength and stability. Similar to this, a strong foundation is necessary for a high-achieving sales team to consistently succeed. Four fundamental pillars support this foundation: technology, coaching, training, and content. Every component is essential to enabling your sales team, increasing income, and advancing your company towards its lofty objectives.

Pillar 1: Content – The Fuel for Sales Conversations

The foundation of sales enablement is content. It gives your sales force the tools they need to interact with potential customers, overcome obstacles, and close deals. Robust content is the cornerstone of establishing reputation, trust, and long-lasting clients.

Key Components of Effective Sales Content:
- **Product Information:** Detailed features, specifications, and descriptions that emphasise the special advantages and value proposition of the product.
- **Case Studies And Customer Stories:** They are actual instances of how your product or service has helped customers and produced desired outcomes.
- **Competitive Battlecards:** Detailed examination of rivals that emphasises your USP and strategies for countering their advantages.
- **Pitches and Presentations For Sales**: presentations and sales scripts that are already created and customised for various buyer profiles and sales phases.
- **Sales Collateral:** Brochures, whitepapers, datasheets, and other marketing documents that aid in closing deals are referred to as sales collateral.

Content Distribution and Management:
You must manage and distribute your material effectively if you want to maximise its impact. Version control and quick access for sales representatives are provided by a centralised content repository. You may analyse content performance and pinpoint areas for improvement by using content analytics.

Think about an abundance of poorly arranged and dispersed sales materials, such as brochures, presentations, and case studies. The key to unlocking this pandemonium is to use Content Management Systems (CMS), which are like hidden gems. You may easily save, arrange, and distribute your sales content with these user-friendly systems. For a tech prospect, do you need a product demo video? An endorsement from a patient for a medical pitch? Your agents can tailor their message and complete more deals when they have access to the ideal information, thanks to a content management system (CMS).

The foundation of contemporary sales enablement is content. However, it might be intimidating to manage a sizable library of material in several formats. Content Management Systems (CMS) are useful in this situation. You may efficiently develop, store, organise, and distribute sales content with the help of these user-friendly tools.

Pillar 2: Training – Sharpening the Sales Arsenal

Good sales training equips representatives with the know-how, abilities, and self-assurance they need to succeed. It's a continuous procedure that guarantees your staff remains up to date with best practices, sales techniques, and product features.

Key Training Components:

- **Product Knowledge:** Comprehensive instruction on the features, advantages, and ways that products solve problems for customers.

- **Sales Methodology**: Educating representatives on tried-and-true sales techniques to organise their sales talks, such as SPIN, Challenger Sale, or Solution Selling.

- **CRM System:** Making sure representatives are adept at managing client data, sales funnels, and forecasts using your CRM system is known as customer relationship management, or CRM training.

- **Communication And Presenting Abilities:** To establish rapport, make compelling pitches, and successfully address objections, one must develop good communication and presenting abilities.

- **Sales Process And Workflow Training:** Educating representatives on the lead qualifying, opportunity management, and deal closing aspects of the company's sales process.

Delivery Methods:

There are several ways to give training, including:

- **Workshops Held In Person:** Led by knowledgeable instructors, they promote interactive learning and knowledge exchange.

- **Online Programmes And Courses**: Adaptable and convenient learning choices for hectic schedules or remote teams.
- **Video-Based Training**: An interesting and eye-catching way to present sales tactics and product demos.
- **Role-Playing Exercises:** Using acquired abilities in real-world sales settings.

Pillar 3: Coaching – Nurturing Sales Excellence

Reps can improve their abilities and overcome obstacles with the help of coaching, which offers customised advice and assistance. It's an ongoing process of skill improvement, observation, and feedback.

Key Coaching Activities:
- **Ride-Alongs And Call Reviews:** Monitoring sales conversations in order to offer immediate feedback and pinpoint areas in need of development.
- **Individualised Coaching Sessions**: Targeted conversations about skill development, goal-setting, and performance.
- **Mentorship Programmes:** Assigning seasoned representatives to more junior team members in order to exchange best practices and information.

- **Performance Reviews And Development Plans:** Making customised development plans for each representative and giving regular performance reviews.

Coaching Tools and Technologies:

Coaching tools including call recording, analytics, and coaching modules are frequently included in sales enablement solutions. These tools can improve teaching efficiency and offer insightful data on representative performance. Platforms for sales enablement are more than just content repositories. Numerous have statistics and call recording as integrated coaching tools. These evaluate rep performance and point up advantages and disadvantages. Think of your sales manager as a superhero because these tools provide salespeople the X-ray vision to see areas that need work and give them the tools they need to succeed. Gong, Outreach, and Salesforce Einstein Conversation Insights are a few well-liked choices.

Pillar 4: Technology – The Catalyst for Efficiency and Insights

The foundation of contemporary sales enablement is technology. Sales representatives are given the resources they require to be effective, efficient, and data-driven.

Key Technology Components:

- **CRM Systems:** They are centralised databases that manage the sales pipeline, store customer information, and facilitate forecasting. One of the most popular example is Salesforce.

- **Platforms For Facilitating Sales:** Easy access to coaching resources, training materials, and sales content. Commonly used Sales Enablement tools are Highspot, Mindtickle, GTM Buddy and Showpad.

- **Tools For Sales Automation:** Automating data input, lead nurturing, and email campaigns are examples of repetitive processes.

- **Mobile Sales Apps:** Giving sales representatives mobile access to CRM data, sales content, and customer information.

- **Tools For Reporting And Analytics In Sales:** Tracking patterns, evaluating results, and offering suggestions for development.

Technology: The Backbone of Modern Sales Enablement

These days, technology is the essential foundation of modern sales enablement. It is the impetus behind data-driven decision-making, rep empowerment, and the transformation of sales processes. Technology increases sales enablement efforts' impact by enabling collaboration, automating processes, and offering real-time analytics.

1. Enhancing Sales Efficiency:

The foundation of efficient sales operations is technology. Together, sales automation technologies, CRM software, and sales enablement platforms remove labor-intensive, manual operations from the business.

- **Automation of Repetitive Tasks:** Sales representatives can concentrate on strategic interactions by automating repetitive tasks like data entry, lead qualifying, and email campaigns.
- **Workflow Optimisation:** With the use of technology, effective workflows can be created, guaranteeing smooth transitions between sales phases and minimising bottlenecks.
- **Content Management:** Reps can easily access the appropriate resources at the appropriate time by using centralised content repositories, which saves them important search time.

2. Empowering Sales Effectiveness:

Technology provides sales representatives with the information and resources they need to succeed.

- **Real-Time Information Access:** Sales enablement technologies give representatives immediate access to competitive analysis, customer information, and product details, allowing them to effectively respond to client requests.

- **Personalised Customer Experiences:** Sales representatives can customise their encounters with customers to suit their unique requirements and preferences by utilising data analytics and Digital Sales Room.
- **Content Optimisation:** By identifying high-performing content, technology-driven analytics enable ongoing enhancement and optimisation of sales collateral.

3. Boosting Sales Productivity:

Technology dramatically increases sales productivity by giving salespeople the tools they need and automating tedious processes.

- **Mobile Enablement:** By enabling sales representatives to access vital information and complete necessary tasks while on the go, sales apps and mobile-optimized platforms boost their productivity and responsiveness.
- **Sales Forecasting and Quota Management**: Sales managers can more efficiently allocate resources, set reasonable quotas, and monitor performance with the aid of sophisticated analytics and forecasting technologies. Popular examples include Clari, Zendesk and Mediafly.
- **Gamification and Incentives:** By using technology to develop captivating and inspiring incentive schemes and sales competitions. Gamification can improve team morale and performance.

4. Driving Data-Driven Decision Making:

The basis of data-driven sales strategy is technology.

- **Sales Analytics:** Cutting-edge analytics systems offer useful information about consumer behaviour, market trends, and sales performance.
- **Predictive Analytics:** Sales enablement technologies can forecast customer behaviour, spot sales opportunities, and streamline sales procedures by examining past data.
- **Data-Driven Personalisation:** By using consumer data to customise product recommendations, content, and messaging, technology makes it possible to create highly personalised sales experiences.

Remember: Technology is not a standalone solution. It's most effective when integrated seamlessly with the other pillars of sales enablement: content, training, and coaching.

Building a Strategic Framework: Blueprint for Sales Success

Consider building a skyscraper. Although a solid foundation is necessary, building would be disorganised and prone to collapsing in the absence of a comprehensive layout. Similar to this, for content, coaching, training, and technology to be the cornerstones of sales enablement, a strategic framework is necessary. To create a framework, it is important to align your business objectives.

It is important to decide where you want to go before getting too technical with your strategy. What are your main objectives as a business? Which goals are you pursuing: more sales, gaining market share, or higher levels of customer satisfaction? Every part of your sales enablement approach will be guided by your well defined objectives.

Let's take a look at "GrowthGear," a B2B software firm that specialises in customer relationship management (CRM) solutions for the healthcare sector. Their main objective for the upcoming fiscal year is to gain 20% more market share. In order to achieve this goal, their sales enablement strategy will give special attention to content that tackles the particular difficulties faced by healthcare organisations, as well as training representatives on rules that are unique to their sector and giving them the resources they need to interact with a variety of decision-makers within healthcare facilities.

When it comes to an effective sales enablement plan, it has to be tailored to meet the requirements of the clients.

The foundation of any effective sales enablement programme is a thorough comprehension of the client. You may better customise your training, sales, and content to appeal to the unique requirements and preferences of your target audience by developing thorough buyer personas.

Let's go back to our previous example, TechNova, a B2B software company. TechNova may customise its content, training, and sales strategy to each manufacturing business segment's specific pain issues and decision-making process by creating thorough buyer personas for small and large-scale manufacturers, for example. This degree of customisation improves the client experience and raises the possibility of successful transactions.

The next question that comes into picture is how to create content that fits well in your sales plan.

No content is produced in a vacuum. Verify that sales, product marketing, and customer success are in sync before publishing. This ideal teamwork makes sure that material meets the demands of customers (sales), aligns with product marketing messaging (product marketing), and gives representatives the tools they need to resolve issues (customer success). Content produced using this cohesive strategy converts, informs, and eventually boosts revenue.

The lifeblood of contemporary sales is content. Creating product sheets and brochures is not enough; you also need to create a content ecosystem that supports the buyer's journey from start to finish.

Envision a thriving market where various forms of content meet the varied demands of consumers. Your sales staff can handle different customer preferences and stages of the sales cycle with the help of a robust content library, which includes engaging blog pieces, educational whitepapers, interactive product demos, webinars and case studies.

For instance, "StyleCraze," a B2C fashion retailer, might produce interesting video tutorials on styling advice, write blog entries about the newest trends in fashion, and provide tailored product recommendations based on client preferences. Customers are further down the sales funnel by this content ecosystem, which inspires, engages, and informs them in addition to informing them.

Here are three things that can help you build a better sales force.

1. **Empowering Your Sales Force: Training and Coaching for Success**

A strong and driven sales staff is the foundation of any prosperous company. A thorough training and coaching programme that gives sales representatives the abilities, know-how, and self-assurance they need to succeed should be a part of your sales enablement plan.

Consider your sales staff to be a top-tier athletic group. Peak performance requires individualised coaching, frequent training sessions, and opportunity for skill growth. By supporting the development of your team, you not only develop each member's potential but also promote a continual improvement culture.

2. Leveraging Technology: Your Sales Copilot

Technology is the unsung hero of modern sales enablement. It streamlines processes, provides valuable insights, and empowers reps to be more efficient.

Consider a CRM system as the central nervous system of your sales organization. It houses customer data, tracks sales activities, and provides valuable insights into sales performance. When integrated with sales enablement platforms, it becomes a powerful tool for delivering the right content to the right rep at the right time.

Here are some important tools that help:

- Customer relationship management, or CRM, systems act as the conductor, making sure everything happens on schedule. CRMs, such as Salesforce, facilitate seamless operation across the sales cycle by centralising customer data, managing the sales pipeline, and tracking interactions.
- Sales Enablement Platforms is your team's go-to resource for information and expertise, like vocal coaches. Reps may deliver powerful messages by using platforms like Highspot or MindTickle, which give them access to training materials, content libraries, and coaching insights.
- Sound engineers are conversational intelligence tools because they record and analyse music. Managers can find areas for improvement by using tools like Chorus.ai and Gong, which record and analyse sales calls and provide

insightful information about the effectiveness of sales representatives.

- Financial analysts are one of the sales forecasting tools; they can predict the revenue rhythm. Sales data is used by QuotaWave and Clari, among other tools, to more accurately forecast revenue streams and anticipate future performance.

- Tools for generating leads locate and draw in possible clients. In order to guarantee a consistent flow of leads, platforms such as 6Sense or LinkedIn Sales Navigator assist you in identifying the ideal customer base for your good or service.

A strong ecosystem that expedites each step of the sales process is created by combining various technologies into a unified tech stack. Your sales force can achieve consistent success with the correct technology combination, which enables everything from lead generation and coaching to deal forecasting and performance analysis.

3. Measuring and Optimizing: The Feedback Loop

A successful sales enablement strategy is not a one-time endeavor; it's an ongoing process of measurement, optimization, and improvement. By tracking key metrics like sales cycle length, win rates, and customer satisfaction, you can identify areas for improvement and refine your strategy accordingly.

Imagine a sales dashboard that provides real-time insights into sales performance. By analyzing this data, you can identify which content pieces are resonating with customers, which sales reps require additional training, and which sales methodologies are driving the best results. This data-driven approach allows you to make informed decisions and continuously optimize your sales enablement efforts.

Remember, building a successful sales enablement framework is a journey, not a destination. It requires ongoing commitment, collaboration, and a willingness to adapt to changing market dynamics. By focusing on these key elements - aligning with business objectives, understanding your customers, creating a robust content ecosystem, empowering your sales team, and leveraging technology – you can build a sales enablement program that drives sustainable growth and positions your organization for long-term success.

Chapter 4: Mastering the Sales Process

Sarah was thinking about a busy market that is brimming with possible buyers. Every customer has a different route, one that involves researching, evaluating, and ultimately making a purchase. Her sales team will be guided by the sales funnel, which functions as a map to help them navigate this busy marketplace and successfully guide customers towards a successful transaction.

Her sales team requires a disciplined method to navigate the complicated geography of client contacts, just like an explorer uses a map and a compass to navigate unknown territory. This crucial road map is provided by the sales funnel, which describes the several phases that buyers must go through before deciding what to buy.

Her sales team follows the sales process as a guide from the first contact with a prospect to the completion of a deal. It's a methodical technique that guarantees efficiency, consistency, and a greater likelihood of closing sales. A thorough understanding of the customer's journey and the steps they go through prior to making a purchase choice is fundamental to this process.

The Anatomy of a Sales Funnel

Consider a funnel. A smaller but highly qualified group converts into paying customers at the bottom, while a large pool of potential customers is available at the top. The sales process is well described by this metaphor of a funnel.

The SaaS sales process is a meticulously planned route that takes prospective clients from awareness to devoted supporters. The main phases are broken down as follows:

1. Drawing in Audience for Lead Generation:

- Targeting and Prospecting: Using focused marketing initiatives, identify the ideal client profile and locate the appropriate prospects.
- With inbound marketing, you can draw in new clients by offering useful material such as blog entries, webinars, and social media interaction.
- Outbound Marketing: Use social selling techniques, cold calling, or email campaigns to make direct contact with qualified prospects.

2. Lead Qualification: Determining the Appropriate Fit

- First Contact: Make a lasting impression by reaching out in a way that piques curiosity and builds rapport.
- BANT Qualification: BANT stands for Budget, Authority, Need and Timeline It is used to make sure the prospect is a

suitable fit for your product, consider their budget, authority to make decisions, unique needs, and urgency.

- Lead scoring: To rank leads with the highest conversion potential, assign points based on prospect behaviour and demographics.

3. Need Analysis: Comprehending the Difficulty

- Discovery Call: Have a thorough discussion to learn about the prospect's objectives, problems, and pain areas.
- Problem Identification: Collaborate with others to identify the precise issues that your solution can resolve.
- Solution Alignment: Explain how your SaaS solution meets the needs that have been defined and provides real benefits.

4. Presentation of the Proposal and Solution (Highlighting the Value):

- Scheduling a Demo: Arrange a product demonstration based on the unique requirements and use cases of the prospect.
- Custom Proposal: Write a strong proposal that includes the value proposition, the cost breakdown, and the main advantages for the particular client.
- Handling Objections: Be prepared for and skillfully respond to any worries or objections that the prospect may voice.

5. Assessment and Choice (The Last Obstacle):

- Follow-up: Stay in constant contact, respond to inquiries right away, and show that you are invested in their achievement.
- Conceptual Proof (POC): To dispel any remaining uncertainties and demonstrate the product's functionality, offer a brief trial or pilot programme.
- Negotiations: In negotiations, both parties should strive cooperatively to reach a mutually beneficial agreement that satisfies their needs.

6. Sealing the Deal (Closing):

- Completed Proposal: Deliver a completed proposal that complies with all agreed-upon terms and conditions.
- Signing the Contract: Put the agreement in writing with a signed contract to formalise it and set the stage for a fruitful collaboration.
- Payment Processing: Simplify the procedure to guarantee a seamless and satisfying client encounter.

7. Relationship-Building Through Implementation and Onboarding:

- Kickoff Meeting: Outline roles and duties, establish clear expectations, and make plans for a smooth implementation.
- Training and Support: Ensure that the customer's staff has received thorough training so they can utilise the SaaS solution to its full potential.

- Customer Success Plan: Create a personalised onboarding and success plan that maximises the customer's investment.

8. Building Loyalty through Post-Sales Engagement and Expansion:
- Consumer input: proactively look for input to pinpoint areas in need of development and raise consumer contentment.
- Upselling and cross-selling: Look for chances to provide new features or services that cater to changing client demands.
- Renewal and Retention: To ensure ongoing income growth, create plans to cultivate enduring partnerships and promote contract renewals.

You can turn the SaaS sales journey into a successful pipeline by grasping these stages and iteratively improving your strategy. This will help you draw in qualified leads, close transactions quickly, and build a devoted clientele that fuels growth and recurring income.

The Evolution of the Sales Funnel: Beyond the Traditional Model

- **The Awareness Stage**: In this stage, potential customers become aware of your product. It means creating blog posts, content for social media, and webinars that captivate and maintain the interest of your target audience.

- **The Phase of Thought:** Prospective customers are considering their options and investigating different strategies during this stage. Providing educational resources like whitepapers, case studies, and product demos can help you differentiate yourself from the competition.

- **The Decision Stage:** At this point, clients are prepared to buy. Customer testimonials, pricing details, and product demonstrations are examples of effective sales enablement that can sway their choice.

- **The Loyalty Stage**: Developing enduring connections with customers is essential to generating referrals and repeat business. Customer feedback systems, loyalty programmes, and post-purchase assistance are crucial elements of this phase.

Now that you know everything there is to know about the sales processing, let us find out how to master it.

Mastering the Sales Process: Popular Methodologies

While knowing the steps of the sales funnel is important, what really sets successful sales teams apart are the particular actions you take at each stage. Over time, a multitude of sales processes have surfaced, each providing unique approaches and methods for successfully navigating the sales process. Now let's examine a few of the most well-liked ones:

SPIN Selling

Popularized by Neil Rackham's book of the same name, SPIN Selling focuses on the types of questions sales reps ask. The acronym stands for:

- **Situation questions:** Understanding the prospect's current situation and environment.
- **Problem questions:** Identifying specific pain points or challenges the prospect faces.
- **Implication questions:** Helping the prospect understand the consequences of the problem.
- **Need-payoff questions:** Connecting the solution to the prospect's desired outcome.

Asking the correct questions to identify the underlying needs of the prospect and illustrating how your product or service effectively answers those needs are key components of SPIN Selling.

Challenger Sale

Traditional consultative sales methods are challenged by the Challenger Sale methodology, which was made popular by Matthew Dixon and Brent Adamson. It suggests that clients desire someone who can question their assumptions and present an alternative viewpoint more than they necessarily want a connection builder.

- Teach: By teaching clients about issues they might not be aware of, challengers take on the role of teachers.
- Tailored: They show a thorough comprehension of the client's industry and customise their solution to meet their unique needs.
- Take charge: In sales conversations, challengers frequently assume the initiative and lead the client towards a solution.

This style works especially well in B2B sales environments that are complex and where customers enjoy a consultative approach that offers valuable insights.

MEDDIC

MEDDIC is a sales qualification methodology primarily used in the technology industry. It stands for:

- **Metrics:** Quantifiable goals the customer wants to achieve.
- **Economic buyer:** The person who controls the budget.
- **Decision criteria:** The factors influencing the purchase decision.
- **Decision process:** The steps involved in the buying process.
- **Identify pain:** Understanding the specific problems the customer is trying to solve.
- **Champion:** The internal advocate for your product or service.

MEDDIC provides a structured framework for qualifying leads and understanding the complex dynamics of B2B sales.

Solution Selling

This customer-focused strategy emphasises pinpointing the unique issues that the prospect faces and positioning your good or service as the best way to address them. It places a strong emphasis on comprehending the business objectives of the client and matching your solution with their intended results.

Consultative selling

This approach, which is related to solution selling, presents the salesman as a reliable counsellor who collaborates with the client to identify problems and suggest customised solutions. It entails determining needs, establishing trusting connections with clients, and actively listening.

The Sandler Selling System

It places a strong emphasis on establishing rapport and controlling the sales dialogue. It focuses on using effective questioning strategies to identify consumer demands and using a cooperative problem-solving approach to overcome objections.

Value Selling

This approach emphasises your product or service's measurable value proposition. It focuses on the return on investment (ROI) and the quantifiable impact your product produces, going beyond features and benefits. Value selling gives sales representatives the tools they need to explain how your solution might save costs, boost productivity, or potentially generate income.

NEAT Selling

This is an abbreviation that stands for Needs, Economic Justification, Authority to Buy, and Timeline. NEAT Selling places a strong emphasis on qualifying leads according to these four essential standards: making sure they have the financial means to make a purchase, the power to make decisions, and a clear need.

Which method should you pick?

For some sales teams, a hybrid strategy that incorporates elements of multiple methodologies to build a tailored sales process may be beneficial. For instance, you may employ MEDDIC to properly validate leads, SPIN questioning to ascertain the needs of the consumer, and Challenger Sale tactics to inform the buyer about possible issues.

The final goal is to choose a procedure that allows your sales team to build strong relationships with customers, understand their needs, and effectively communicate the advantages of your product or service.

Recall that although these approaches offer a strong basis, there is no one-size-fits-all strategy for the sales process. The secret to success is adaptability and flexibility.

After you have selected the right sales method for yourself, you also need to ensure that it aligns with the enablement strategies.

Aligning Sales Methodologies with Enablement Strategies

Though it's only the first stage, choosing the appropriate sales tactic is essential. It must be easily included into your sales enablement plan in order to have the greatest possible impact. This alignment guarantees that your sales staff has the resources, training, and information needed to apply the technique successfully. Here are some aspects that you must keep in mind when aligning the sales methods with the enablement strategies:

Content Alignment

- SPIN Selling: Content should focus on addressing specific customer problems and demonstrating the value of your solution. Whitepapers, case studies, and ROI calculators can be particularly effective in this context.

- Challenger Sale: Your content should establish your business as a thought leader and offer analysis of current market trends and pressing issues. Research reports, webinars, and expert articles might all fall under this category.

- MEDDIC: Content should be tailored to address the specific decision criteria of your target customers. Case studies highlighting how your product or service meets these criteria can be highly effective.

- Solution selling: It places a strong emphasis on identifying the unique problems that your customers are facing and positioning your product as the best way to solve them. Testimonials and customer success stories show actual instances of how your product has assisted related firms in overcoming challenges and succeeding. The value proposition of your solution is strengthened by this content's social proof and trust-building qualities.

- NEAT Selling: The focus of NEAT Selling is on certifying leads according to predetermined standards. Content that highlights typical problems and obstacles in the business can assist potential customers in identifying their own needs. Budget justification tools also enable prospects to comprehend the financial advantages of your solution and present a compelling internal investment case. The qualification process is streamlined by this tailored content, which draws leads with strong purchase intent and who fulfil the profile.

Training Alignment

- SPIN Selling: Sales training should emphasize question-asking techniques, active listening, and the ability to uncover customer pain points. Role-playing exercises can be used to practice SPIN questioning scenarios.

- Challenger Sale: Training ought to concentrate on honing the abilities required to instruct clients about novel issues and their fixes. Sales representatives must possess the skills necessary to make persuasive presentations and handle objections.

- MEDDIC: The process of qualifying leads utilising the MEDDIC framework, which includes identifying key decision-makers, comprehending their purchasing criteria, and identifying their pain areas, should be included in training.

- Solution selling: It includes consultative selling strategies, cooperative problem-solving approaches, and presentation customisation to meet unique client needs. Role-playing games can be created to mimic real-world situations in which salespeople collaborate with potential customers to jointly develop solutions.

- Value selling: This is the process of outlining your product's measurable value proposition, estimating return on investment, and creating strong business justifications. Workshops on data analysis, financial modelling, and creating compelling presentations that highlight the

quantifiable advantages your product offers can all be
included in training.

Technology Alignment

- SPIN Selling: Sales enablement technology should facilitate
  effective communication and collaboration. Sales
  representatives can acquire information and cultivate
  relationships with prospects with the aid of tools like as
  content management platforms, email automation, and
  CRM systems.

- Challenger Sale: Technology can facilitate the Challenger
  approach by giving access to data-driven insights,
  competition intelligence, and industry research. Delivering
  personalised presentations and material is another usage for
  sales enablement platforms.

- MEDDIC: By automating data gathering and analysis,
  technology can facilitate the lead qualification process. Key
  performance indicators and opportunities can be found by
  using CRM systems and technologies for sales automation.

- Solution Selling: To obtain client information and industry
  insights, sales intelligence tools can be utilised. This gives
  sales representatives the ability to customise their strategy,
  spot buying signals, and modify their offers to fit the unique
  requirements and circumstances of each client.
  Furthermore, cooperative technologies such as video
  conferencing software and document sharing platforms can

help in cooperative problem-solving and solution co-creation with potential clients.

- Value Selling: ROI calculators and cost-benefit analysis tools can be found on sales enablement platforms. With the help of these interactive tools, representatives may work in real-time with prospects while demonstrating the quantifiable effects of your product on their company. Furthermore, sales data and analytics solutions can offer insightful information about the behaviour and purchasing patterns of customers, allowing representatives to customise their value propositions and sales tactics for optimum effect.

In many cases, a hybrid approach combining elements of different sales methodologies can be most effective. For example, you might use SPIN questioning to uncover customer needs, then apply Challenger Sale techniques to position your solution as a unique and valuable offering.

Aligning Sales Methodology with Buyer Personas
Another critical aspect of alignment is considering your buyer personas. Different buyer segments may respond better to different sales methodologies. For instance, a technical buyer might appreciate a more data-driven, Challenger-style approach, while a relationship-oriented buyer might respond better to a consultative, SPIN-based approach.

Sales Enablement Playbooks

To ensure consistent execution of your chosen sales methodology, consider creating sales enablement playbooks. These playbooks outline specific steps, content, and tools required for each stage of the sales process. For example, an SPIN Selling playbook could include a template for crafting effective situation questions, a list of case studies to demonstrate problem-solving techniques, and guidelines for handling common objections.

A strong sales team is built on the foundation of a well-written sales enablement playbook. It's a thorough manual that gives your sales representatives the information, abilities, and resources they need to successfully negotiate the sales process on a regular basis. The essential elements usually present in a sales enablement playbook are broken down as follows:

1. Introduction:
- Set the stage by outlining the purpose and importance of the playbook.
- Briefly introduce your company, its mission, and its core values.

2. Sales Team Structure:
- Define the different roles within your sales team (e.g., SDRs, Account Executives, Sales Engineers) and their respective responsibilities.

3. Sales Methodology:

- Outline the chosen sales methodology (e.g., SPIN, Challenger, MEDDIC) and explain its core principles.
- Provide guidance on how to apply the methodology throughout the sales cycle.

4. Target Market:

- Clearly define your ideal customer profile (ICP), including demographics, firmographics, and buying behaviors.
- Offer insights into your target market's needs, challenges, and pain points.

5. Value Proposition:

- Articulate your unique value proposition (UVP) - what makes your product or service stand out from the competition?
- Explain how your solution addresses the specific needs of your target market and delivers tangible benefits.

6. Lead Generation:

- Outline various lead generation strategies, both inbound and outbound.
- Provide guidance on qualifying leads and prioritizing them based on fit and potential value.

7. Sales Script and Templates:

- Offer basic sales scripts and email templates to ensure consistent messaging across your sales team.
- Emphasize the importance of personalization and tailoring communication to specific customer needs.

8. Objection Handling:

- Anticipate common objections raised by prospects and equip your reps with effective rebuttal strategies.
- Offer frameworks and techniques for confidently navigating objections and turning them into selling opportunities.

9. Proposal and Closing:

- Provide guidance on crafting compelling proposals that showcase the value proposition and address customer needs.
- Offer strategies for effective closing techniques and securing deals.

10. Pricing:

- Explain your pricing structure and different pricing models (e.g., subscription, tiered pricing).
- Equip reps with the knowledge to handle pricing inquiries and negotiate effectively.

11. Sales Tools and Technologies:

- List and explain the different sales enablement tools and technologies available to your team (e.g., CRM, sales intelligence platforms, content management systems).
- Guide reps on how to leverage these tools to maximize their productivity and sales performance.

12. Metrics & KPIs:

- Define key performance indicators (KPIs) that track the effectiveness of your sales process. (e.g., conversion rates, lead generation metrics, sales cycle length).
- Encourage continuous monitoring and analysis of these metrics to identify areas for improvement.

13. Onboarding and Training:

- Outline the onboarding process for new sales reps, ensuring they are equipped with the necessary knowledge and skills.
- Detail ongoing training programs to keep your team up-to-date on industry trends, product updates, and best practices.

14. Customer Success and Retention:

- Emphasize the importance of customer success and building long-term relationships.
- Offer strategies for delivering exceptional customer service and fostering ongoing engagement.

15. Compliance and Legal:

- Provide information on any relevant compliance regulations or legal requirements that your sales team needs to be aware of.
- Offer guidance on ethical sales practices and ensuring data privacy compliance.

Remember: This is a general framework, and the specific components of your sales enablement playbook may vary depending on your company's size, industry, and sales process. Regularly review and update your playbook to ensure it remains relevant and reflects the evolving needs of your sales team and market dynamics.

By providing a clear roadmap and equipping your sales reps with the necessary resources, your sales enablement playbook empowers your team to navigate the sales journey with confidence, convert leads into loyal customers, and drive sustainable sales growth.

To understand this better

If you want to be sure that your sales enablement activities are yielding the expected results, it is imperative that you monitor key performance indicators (KPIs) and make data-driven improvements. Key performance indicators (KPIs) such as win rates, sales cycle time, and client satisfaction should be tracked in order to assess the effectiveness of your sales process and enablement strategies.

When you combine your enablement strategy with your sales methodology, you have a potent mix that enables your sales force to produce outstanding outcomes. Recall that the keys are adaptation and flexibility. Keep assessing and improving your strategy to make sure it fits the changing needs of your clients and the state of the industry.

A good sales plan starts with an understanding of the sales funnel and the processes that direct it. Sales teams can precisely navigate the complicated environment of client contacts by using customised tactics and segmenting the customer journey into discrete segments.

The SPIN, Challenger, Solution Selling, Consultative Selling, Sandler Selling System, Value Selling, NEAT Selling and MEDDIC approaches provide useful frameworks for organising sales talks and successfully meeting client needs. However, the best strategy is usually a hybrid model that combines aspects of these approaches to fit your target market's and your sales team's unique requirements.

Recall that the sales process is not a set procedure. It's a dynamic structure that needs to be adjusted and improved upon constantly. Your selected technique and sales enablement plan should work together to generate a potent force that increases revenue. The capacity to assess and optimise your sales performance, together with having a well-trained sales team and a thorough grasp of your clients, are ultimately what will determine your level of success.

Chapter 5: Needs Assessment and Goal Setting

Effective sales enablement program begins with a good grasp of your organisation's particular challenges and aspirations. Needs assessment and setting clear, measurable goals are key starting points for a results-driven program.

Conducting a comprehensive needs assessment

A successful sales enablement program starts with a deep understanding of your organisation's needs. It uncovers gaps, challenges, and opportunities that exist within a sales team and presents the foundation upon which a targeted and effective strategy can be designed. Here are some things that you must keep in mind-

- **Identifying Pain Points:** First, pinpoint precisely what problems your sales force is facing. This will mean drilling down into daily operations to find bottlenecks and, more critically, understanding their greatest frustrations.

- **Sales Performance:** Checking parameters like win rates, sales cycle length, or customer acquisition cost can give insights into how to change. A low conversion rate or longer sales cycles might indicate the need for more product knowledge or improved selling skills.
- **Inefficiencies in the Sales Process:** Map out the current sales process to identify bottleneck points and redundancy. Slow lead qualification or very long time to create proposals may point to inefficiencies that need resolution.
- **Technology Gaps:** Take an inventory of the current sales technology stack. Are your sales reps equipped with what they need to win? Outdated systems or lack of some functionality can weigh heavily on productivity and net sales performance.
- **Content Effectiveness:** Assess the quality and relevance of your current sales content. Is it attuned to buyer personas and really aiding the process of sales? Past or irrelevant content can inhibit sales reps from properly engaging prospects.
- **Sales Team Capabilities:** Evaluate your sales team for knowledge, skills, and training. Are there particular gaps within the team around objection handling or negotiation that need to be attended to?

To help you understand the needs better, you need to establish better data collection methods.

Data Collection Methods

This would require all, or some of the following measures for comprehensive data collection:

- **Questionnaires and surveys:** Take feedback from sales representatives, sales managers, and customers
- **In-depth interviews:** Have personal interviews with top stakeholders to gain profound insights
- **Analysis of sales data:** Analyze the sales performance metrics against pre-defined sales trends and patterns
- **Audit sales process:** Observe sales interactions and analyze sales documents.

These methods can be combined to create an all-inclusive picture of the needs and challenges faced by your sales team. By conducting a needs assessment, you will hear the active voice of your sales team and gather data from various sources.

The insights learned through this process will serve as the foundation on which to formulate a focussed sales enablement strategy that deals with specific pain points and can actually drive measurable results. Thus, coming into picture is your next step, setting of the SMART goals.

Setting SMART Goals for Your Sales Enablement Program

Having gained a deep understanding of what your sales team needs, it becomes only logical that such insights be translated into actionable goals. These SMART goals will take clear guidance from your sales enablement program and ensure focus, with alignment to broader business objectives.

- **Specific:** Clearly state what you want to attain. Try to avoid general goals or those that are too vague. Instead of saying, "Improve sales productivity," say, "Reduce average sales cycle length by 10%."
- **Measurable:** Define how you will know when you hit your goal. Specify what quantifiable metrics you are going to use to define success. If you're looking to improve the win rates for sales reps, define how you'll measure wins, like by deals closed or revenue generated.
- **Attainable**: Setting challenging but realistic goals needs to take into account any team's potential capabilities, available resources, and the conditions in the market. Overly ambitious goals will bring frustration and demotivating individuals.
- **Relevant:** Make sure your goal relates to the overall business objectives. Your sales enablement efforts need to make some contribution towards the overall success of the

company. For example, if your company is focused on expanding into new markets, then your sales enablement goals should support market penetration efforts.

- **Time-bound:** The goal needs to specify when it shall be realized. This builds urgency and holds one responsible. Larger goals are broken down into smaller milestones with specific timelines to track progress.

Example of SMART Sales Enablement Goals:
- In six months, raise the average deal size by around 5% by emphasising product knowledge and sales skill development.
- Create a new lead qualification procedure and make use of the sales automation tools that are now available to reduce the time of the sales cycle by around 7%.
- By giving the sales representatives improved sales content and coaching programs, you can increase their win rate by around 12%.
- Improved post-sale assistance and customer success programs can raise customer satisfaction ratings by around 10%.

In order to measure the sales enablement program's performance over time and make data-driven adjustments, it is imperative to set clear, measurable targets. Always make sure that your goals are relevant and align with the overarching strategic objectives of your company. Make sure that your aims are both tough and reachable.

Once you have set your goals, you need a great team and stakeholders to execute them well.

Key Stakeholders Identification

A successful sales enablement program requires active contributions from many other parts of the organization. To guarantee that the program has buy-in and actual value is added, that it remains in line with larger organisational objectives, and that it solves more business pain areas, key stakeholders must be identified and included. Sales managers, sales leaders, and frontline sales personnel are the main participants in this exercise. The sales team's understanding of the issues they face is crucial for developing a sales enablement plan.

- **Product Team:** The product team provides specific knowledge about the product or service a company sells, such as features and benefits. It is key to developing powerful sales messaging and related content.
- **Marketing Team:** Lead generation is greatly aided by the marketing team, which also supplies sales with all the necessary materials. The marketing staff can offer knowledge in areas such as consumer segmentation, message, and branding.
- **Customer Success:** This team brings a different, valuable perspective regarding the needs and expectations of customers. Their insights will be very instrumental in

tailoring sales enablement efforts around customer satisfaction and retention.

- **Executive Leadership:** The executive team provides strategic direction entailing alignment with overall business objectives. Their support is instrumental in working to ensure the appropriate resourcing and prioritization for the sales enablement initiative.

To help foster effective collaboration, consider these strategies:

- **Cross-functional workshops**: To bring together key stakeholders across departments to discuss challenges, share insights, and brainstorm solutions.
- **Joint goal setting**: Setting up common objectives and KPIs aligned with overall business goals.
- **Regular communication:** Establish regular communication channels for sharing information and collaboration.
- **Shared ownership:** Build a shared ownership of the sales enablement program by taking them along in the decision-making process.

Engage your key stakeholders at the beginning, and you will be off to a great sales enablement program. Their insights, know-how, and buy-in will help drive your program toward success.

Chapter 6: Crafting Your Sales Enablement Strategy

Knowing exactly what your sales team needs and where you want to go, it is time to build a comprehensive Sales Enablement strategy. This chapter will walk you through creating a roadmap that aligns your efforts in the right direction toward your overall business objectives.

A sales enablement strategy is far more than a lot of tactics strung together; it's a roadmap to guide your salesforce to its potential. Based on the unique needs of your organization, you should be able to create a strategy that produces measurable outcomes.

Let's begin with the most important components that build up to a successful sales enablement strategy.

Developing a Strategic Framework

An organized approach is called for in developing a great sales enablement strategy. The SWOT framework identifies important internal company strengths and weaknesses with external opportunities and threats.

SWOT Analysis for Sales Enablement

- **Strengths**: Identify core strengths of your sales team, with respect to availability of resources and efforts taken, that have led them to success. This may include good sales culture, strong sales leadership, or a proven track record in a particular market segment.
- **Weakness:** Identifying the weakness in your sales enablement strategy can help you understand where exactly you or your team is going wrong. This can be in terms of the wrong target group or simply implying the right strategy at the wrong time.
- **Opportunities:** Think of the external factors that can favor them, such as new technologies, changed market trends, and unexplored customer bases.
- **Threats**: Anything that may be a hitch or trouble for sales like economic lows, higher competition, and changes in regulation.

Upon identifying your SWOT analysis, this would be the time that you would start to devise specific strategies on how to capitalize on your strengths, at the same time bridging weaknesses.

Always remember that a SWOT analysis is like a live document, revised continually based on shifts or transitions in your business environment. The next step after SWOT analysis is to create a proper timeline and set goals to milestones to ensure the plan is followed through.

Creating a Roadmap with Timelines and Milestones

A good sales enablement roadmap is a guide in the delivery of your team to success. It describes the key initiatives, timelines, and resources involved in the achievement of your sales goals. Key components of a sales enablement roadmap include the following:

Clear goals and objectives
- Define desired outcomes: Be specific about what you want to achieve with your sales enablement program. This could relate to how you will increase sales revenue, improve win rates, or shorten sales cycles; or anything that pertains to enhanced customer satisfaction.
- Align with Business Objectives: Be sure that your sales enablement targets directly relate to the broader objectives of your business. This kind of alignment will ensure that

your efforts echo within the larger attainment of business success.

- Set SMART Goals: Definite goals that, in every different aspect, are specific, measurable, achievable, relevant, and bound by a specific timeframe for the enablement strategy.

Key Initiatives

- Content Creation: Describe the development of quality, focused content responsive to customer needs and driving the selling process.
- Sales Training: Define the curriculum, delivery methods, and frequency of sales training programs to skill and knowledge-enhance reps.
- Coaching and Mentoring: Create a coaching/mentoring program that will keep the sales reps continuously supported and open to growth.
- Technology Implementation: Identify and integrate the correct sales enablement tools and platforms that will drive process efficiencies and productivity.

Timelines and Milestones

- Create a Timeline: For each initiative, develop a practical timeline. Do this by breaking large projects into smaller, easy tasks. Set key checkpoints for checking on the progress and ensuring that the project is running as planned. These milestones need to be specific and tied back to the objectives and overall goals.

- Resource Allocation: Determine human and financial resources that would be required for each initiative, together with responsibilities.

Roles and Responsibilities

- Define Roles: Articulate what roles the different teams involved in sales enablement will take on, which often include Sales, Marketing, Product, and Enablement.
- Establish Ownership: Define who will be responsible for every initiative and ensure communication and collaboration are clearly expressed.
- Establish Accountability: Personal and team accountability to commitments and deadlines

Metrics and KPIs

- Identify Key Metrics: Identify the key performance indicators that will measure the success of your sales enablement initiatives. These metrics need to align with your overall business objectives.
- Track Progress: Take regular monitoring and analysis of the KPIs to know the effects of efforts in sales enablement and make data-driven adjustments accordingly.
- Communicate Results: Share performance metrics to express the value of sales enablement to the stakeholders in order to build further support.

Get on this roadmap, and you will have in your hands a very strong sales enablement program that really drives results and helps propel organizational success.

Visualizing Your Roadmap

Put your plan into action by using something visual like a Gantt chart or roadmap software. Visualization will further help in drawing the means of executing your strategy, to communicate and track over time. Here are some things to keep in mind:

- **Flexibility and Adaptation**

Keep in mind that your sales enablement roadmap is a living document. It may require adjustments from time to time, due to changes in organizational evolution and market conditions. Revisit this roadmap regularly for appropriate updates so that it remains relevant towards the attainment of your business objectives. Establishing an action-oriented roadmap provides clear direction and a sense of purpose for your sales team, which shall drive focus and accountability, hence success. Aligning the existing roadmap with the business objectives in a broader sense is equally important.

- **Aligning Enablement with Broader Business Objectives**

A successful sales enablement strategy is not something on one side; it's a part of the business strategy. It holds much potential when aligned with broader organizational goals.

- **Understanding Business Objectives**

It's very important to have a clear understanding of the overarching objectives for your company before getting into specific enablement tactics. These would be some of the key questions:

- What is the mission and vision of the company?
- What are the major revenue drivers?
- What KPIs are used to measure success?
- What are the targets for growth, and what kind of expansion plans does it have?

Having your sales enablement strategy focused on these broader business goals assures that you are working toward the desired outcomes.

Tie Enablement to Business Initiatives:

Once you have a clear understanding of what your business objectives are, then you can start to identify specific areas in which sales enablement can help. For example, market expansion: if it's entering new markets, the sales enablement will equip the sales representatives with the proper knowledge, tools, and content relevant for success in those new territories.

- **Product Launch**: Sales enablement can arm your sales team with information on new products or services being launched so that it can communicate the value proposition effectively to customers and answer all their queries.

- **Customer Retention:** Sales enablement is responsible for customer success, builds solid relationships with them, and thus is able to retain more customers with less churning.

- **Cross-Functional Collaboration:** Inevitably, driving optimal alignment means facilitating collaboration among the sales, marketing, product, and customer success teams. Working together, you can develop a unified approach that gives consistency and drives maximum impact out of sales enablement efforts.

- **Measure and Adjust**: Check frequently that your sales enablement efforts remain aligned with broader business objectives. Track the impact of your work by using KPIs and making adjustments where necessary. You can ensure that your sales enablement program remains relevant to the changing business needs by tracking performance data and further making adjustments.

Tying your sales enablement strategy to these larger business objectives creates that kind of synergy to foster growth, efficiency, and customer satisfaction.

Chapter 7: Building Powerful Training Programs

An organization should aim at continuously developing and improving employees since the nature of today's business environment has a dynamic nature and change has no choice but to occur. Organizations need to give their working people the right qualifications and skills to edify their competitive advantage towards productivity in the industry. Formation of a robust training program is not only to communicate the information but also to make an exciting, effective, and transformative learning experience.

This chapter will cover the basic elements in developing effective training programs. We start with an important stage, that is, curriculum development; it follows a needs assessment to assure that the training will be designed with regard to the needs particular to the participants. The course will then discuss the different approaches to delivery in training, such as in-person, online, or hybrid, and how to choose the best approach in a given context. We will then proceed to create engaging and interactive training content with examples and best practices to understand these concepts in operation.

You should close out this chapter believing that you can, in fact, design and construct training programs that will enhance skills and knowledge and drive a culture of continuous improvement and excellence in your organization.

Curriculum Development Based on Needs Assessment

A good, powerful training program should start with an understanding of the needs of the audience. Needs assessment means determining what exactly in skills, knowledge, and abilities is to be developed in the first place. A good needs assessment drives the training program towards relevance, usefulness, and need-based orientation for those for whom it is being conducted.

Steps in Conducting Needs Assessment

- **Identify the Stakeholders:** Consult all the key stakeholders, namely the management, staff, and subject matter experts. This could include production supervisors, HR managers, and senior management in a manufacturing company.

- **Information Gathering:** This may be done through questionnaires, interviews, focus groups, and observations. For example, this can be achieved by conducting a survey in all the various branches of a retail chain to compile information on customer service skills.

- **Analyze Information**: Analysis of the information gathered with an eye on common themes and areas that need improvement. This could involve statistical analysis to pinpoint where deficiencies in skills may lie or qualitative to gain insight into the nuances of the responses of the employees.

- **Prioritize Needs**: Identified needs have to be prioritized for their impact on the organizational goals. This may mean, in a SaaS company, that training on new product features would be put on a priority as against some other less important skills.

- **Develop Learning Objectives:** Based on the prioritized needs, clear and measurable learning objectives for the program will have to be developed. For example, an objective for a sales training program could be to increase the closing rate.

Choosing the Right Training Delivery Methods

The next step after the needs assessment would be the choice of appropriate training delivery methods. The choice of method here is pegged to various factors, which include the nature of the content, characteristics of the learners, and also the kind and available resources at their disposal. Especially in the Indian context, where there could be vast variations with regard to access to technology and connectivity, methods will have to be chosen so that they are accessible and effective for the audience.

In-Person Training

In this mode of training, instructors and trainees interact face-to-face. It is highly useful for hands-on training, group activities, and feedback on a real-time basis.

Advantages:
- Interactive: Both interactions and feedback are instant.
- Engagement: Conducting group activities and running discussions is much easier.
- Customization: The trainer can change the content as per the reactions and questions from participants.

Online Training

Online training, or e-learning, uses digital means of platforms in delivering the training content. Online training is more suitable in cases where the audience is geographically dispersed and training requiring self-paced learning.

Advantages:
- Flexibility: The participants can access the training materials per their convenience.
- Scalability: Delivering the training to a large number of participants spread across various geographic locations is not at all an arduous task.
- Cost-Effectiveness: Saves traveling and accommodation expenses of the trainees involved in off-site training.

Hybrid Training

Hybrid training combines face-to-face and online modes of training, thus getting the best of both worlds. This may have particular relevance in India, where access to technology varies from one region to another.

Advantages
- Flexibility: Offers flexibility of both face-to-face and online modes of training.

- Adaptability: Can cater to the varied needs of individual participants.
- Engagement: Provides multiple ways for engaging participants with the content.

Creating Engaging and Interactive Training Content

How effective any training program will be rests, to a large extent, on the quality of the content and how engaging and interactive it really is. Good content is engaging and calls learners to active participation in the training.

Principles of Engaging Training Content

- **Relevance:** The content should be relevant to what the learners do. Examples and case studies being used have to resonate very clearly with the given context.

- **Clarity:** Express ideas in simple and clear language. Avoid jargon and technical terms that could be unclear to the learners.
- **Interactivity**: Build interactive components like quizzes, polls, and discussion forums that keep learners interested.

- **Variety:** Use a mix of content types, such as videos, infographics, image shows, and text, to accommodate different learning styles.
- **Practical Application:** Embed practical exercises, simulations, and role-playing activities to enable learners to enact what they have learned.

Use technology

Technology can be used to make the training content interactive and engaging. Tools to be used include Learning Management Systems, which will be helpful in content delivery and tracking progress and feedback provisions. One can use Virtual Reality and Augmented Reality for creating highly immersive experiences in learning.

Example: Technology-Enhanced Training in Manufacturing

An AR application was developed for the machine operators of a manufacturing company in India. With AR glasses, the machine operators were able to see real-time instructions and visual guides overlaid on the equipment, thereby easily understanding any complex procedures. This interactive, immersive approach did not only bring about huge reductions in training time but also enhanced operational efficiency.

Conclusion

Building potent training programs involves a systematic approach: scanning and analyzing continuously to understand the training requirements through proper needs assessment. The choice of appropriate delivery methods ensures access and effectiveness for the target group. Making content interesting and interactive captures the learners' attention and stimulates their learning. Making the life of the training programs more relevant and effective by inter-linking cultural elements with the use of technology. These strategies can hence be adopted in the global context to develop better skills and capabilities of the workforce in organizations for growth and success in a competitive market.

Chapter 8: Leveraging Technology for Sales Enablement

In this fast-moving, competitive world of business, technology in selling is the key to growth and success. Proper sales enablement tools can help increase the productivity and effectiveness of a sales team and create efficient workflows while giving useful insights into decision-making. Using proper tools, integration with other tools, and training for using these technologies are where problems manifest. In the following chapter, we will explain how to choose the right sales enablement tools for your process of estimating and choosing, how to integrate with CRM and marketing automation, and how to train your team to use the technology efficiently.

Evaluating and Selecting the Right Sales Enablement Tools

The selection of the right sales enablement tools involves a rigorous assessment exercise that ensures the tools completely align with the organizational goals and requirements. The right tools will equip your sales team with knowledge, expedite workflows, and ultimately improve customer interactions.

Identifying Your Needs

The starting point in assessing the sales enablement tools is identification of what exactly an organization needs. Take a minute to consider the following questions:

- What are the current problems or pain points for the sales team today?
- What are your sales goals and objectives?
- What kind of features and functionalities will you require for your sales process?
- How will the tools integrate with other systems?

Categorizing Sales Enablement Tools

The sales enablement tools are the backbone to modern sales organizations, helping the sales team become more efficient, effective, and client-centric. Broadly, these can be classified under six categories, viz., CMS system, Sales Training and Coaching, CRM System, Sales Engagement Platforms, Sales Intelligence Tool and Sales Analytics and Reporting.

Content Management System

A Content Management System is a hub of all sales-related content. It provides the backbone needed for a sales team so that it can provide the right materials at the right time; it's also a single source of truth. In most cases, these tools usually offer the following robust features for content creation and storage—from product sheets and case studies to presentations and videos. The main pillars of content management systems are:

- **Content Organization:** This is very critical to its ease of retrieval. CMS tools are available that provide tagging, categorization, and even search functionalities to help the sales rep get to the content quickly.
- **Content Distribution:** Whether it is internal or external distribution of content, the same can be easily done with the aid of CMS platforms through a number of channels, such as email or even social media.
- **Content Analytics:** Be able to track the usage and engagement for content and gain insights into content performance to aid in the optimization of content creation and distribution strategies.

Examples: Seismic, Highspot, Showpad.

Sales Training and Coaching Platforms

Sales training and coaching form two of the integral components of a high-performance sales team. Specialized platforms bring a structured approach to:

- **Onboarding New Hires:** Go higher on the learning curve of new reps through end-to-end training modules on product knowledge, sales process, and company culture.
- **Skill Development:** Continue training and developing reps on changing trends in the industry, sales methodologies, and updates to products.
- **Coaching And Feedback:** Provide managers with tools for real-time coaching and feedback that will help reps improve on their performance.
- **Performance Tracking:** Track the performance of sales reps by using assessments and role-plays, spot the ones that need improvement.

Common examples include Brainshark, Lessonly, and MindTickle.

Sales Analytics and Reporting Tools

Data-driven insights are integral to perfecting sales performance. Sales analytics and reporting tools would make available those data to:

- **Measure Sales Performance:** A way to track sales performance based on metrics like revenue, sales win rates, deal size, and the length of time it takes to close.
- **Identify Patterns/Trends:** The analysis of sales data by a seller allows him/her to identify patterns and trends that help him/her predict future performance and give insight for informed decisions. One can even optimize the sales

process through data analysis in order to identify bottlenecks and inefficiencies in the process of sales.

- **Forecasting Sales:** One can easily develop an accurate sales forecast from historical data and current trends. Popular examples include Salesforce Analytics, Clari, InsightSquared, and Klipfolio.

Customer Relationship Management Systems

A CRM system is the lifeline of any sales organization, offering a single location to store all customer information and interactions. Equipped with this system, sales teams can manage customer data, track opportunities, and automate workflows.

Provide a single view of the customer across the organization for personalized interactions and better customer service to improve customer satisfaction. Popular examples: Salesforce, HubSpot, Zoho CRM.

Sales Intelligence Tools

Today's sales intelligence tools are what a prospector's pickaxe used to be: gadgets that can unearth valuable insights about potential customers. From ZoomInfo, LinkedIn Sales Navigator to Lusha, these platforms have provided a treasure trove of data that allows sales teams to identify, qualify, and engage prospects effectively.

These tools give you detailed company information, contacts, firmographic data, and even buying signals. Armed with this intelligence, you will empower your sales team to personalize outreach, prioritize leads, and increase conversion rates.
Think of Sales Intelligence as a compass that lays down your sales team's navigation course across the ocean of prospect customers into the most promising ones, thereby maximizing their chance of success.

Sales Engagement Platforms

Sales Engagement Platforms are designed to increase sales rep productivity and prospects' engagement. They typically have the following features:

- **Email automation:** Send out personalized email campaigns and automate follow-up activities.
- **Automation of sales sequences:** Create automated sequences of emails, calls, and other activities for lead nurturing.
- **Activity tracking:** Monitor activity levels and performance metrics for sales reps.
- **Coaching:** Provide real-time coaching and guidance based on the behavior of sales reps.

Popular examples include Gong, Outreach, SalesLoft, Groove.

It's through such categories and features that specific differentiators are offered within different tools that sales organizations can select the combination of platforms necessary to drive revenue growth through process optimization.

Evaluating Sales Enablement Tools

Once you have identified what your needs are and the kinds of tools available in the market, it's time for the evaluation process. Begin from an understanding of the following criteria:

- **Ease of use:** The tool has to be extremely user-friendly and easy to use. Sales teams tend to favor what is more workable and easier to navigate.
- **Integration:** Make sure that the tool integrates very seamlessly into your already existing CRM and marketing automation systems. There is a need to integrate data for consistency and smoothing of workflows.
- **Scalability:** The tool should be such that it scales with your organization. It has to have the capacity to handle an increasing number of users and large amounts of data.
- **Customization:** Customize the tool by looking for tools that offer customization features to tailor their features and functionalities as per your requirements.

- **Support And Training:** Assess the support and training provided by the vendor. Proper support will ensure that problems are dealt with in no time, while training enables your team to get up to speed regarding the usage of the new tool.
- **Cost:** Do not forget about the cost of the tool. This includes all implementation and maintenance costs involved. Ensure it fits within your budget and that it provides good value for money spent.

Example: Choice of Sales Enablement Platforms

Let's take the example of an Indian pharmaceutical company facing a challenge in enhancing its sales content management. When the need for a central platform to manage and distribute sales content becomes undeniable, the company selects a few sales enablement platforms for evaluation. In their minds, they have specified ease of use, integration with the existing CRM, and strong features for analytics as paramount. Following proper evaluation, they chose Highspot for its ease of use, tight integration with Salesforce, and depth of analytics. The decision comes right after researching through the different users' positive feedback from within the industry, besides a vendor's strong support and training programs.

Seamless Integration with Existing CRM and Marketing Automation Systems

The ability of technology to integrate is very critical in leveraging the same in sales enablement. This smooth integration ensures that data moves smoothly between different systems, giving a single view of customer interactions for effective decision-making.

Benefits of Integration

Here are some of the benefits of integration:

- **Data Consistency**: Integration enforces consistency in data across all systems. That avoids possible discrepancies and provides everybody within any organization the exact information.
- **Integrated Workflows:** Because of the automation of data transfer and a reduced need for manual data entry, integrated systems really improve workflow efficiency. This increases productivity and minimizes the occurrence of errors.
- **Improved Customer Insight:** Integration offers an overall view of customer contact activities across various touchpoints. It helps to understand customer behavior and preferences better and thus enables more personalized and effective sales strategies.

- **Improved Collaboration:** The integrated systems work toward better collaboration among sales, marketing, and customer support teams. That means everyone is on the same page when working to attain set objectives.

Steps to Integrate Seamlessly

If you want to integrate seamlessly, follow these steps:

- **Check for Compatibility:** You need to make sure the tool for sales enablement you opt for is compatible with your CRM and marketing automation systems. Check if there are pre-built integrations or APIs that allow for data exchange.
- **Define The Integration Requirements:** Be clear about what the integration requirements will be, specifically on shared data and how frequently it will be updated, and the workflows that need to be automated.
- **Select the Right Way to Integrate**: Based on the requirement, the suitable integration approach has to be chosen. It may be direct integration using APIs, middleware solution, or third-party integration platform.
- **Plan the Integration Process:** Develop a plan for integration that details all the steps involved, a timeline, and the resources required. Ensure stakeholders are informed and aligned to the process.
- **Test the Integration:** Test the integration before it goes live for the identification and resolution of issues. The tests

must be end-to-end, which involves confirming that data is flowing and the workflows are running as expected.

- **Monitor and Maintain:** Monitor the performance consistently once it has gone live. Check at regular intervals for any errors and make necessary changes for hassle-free functioning.

Example: Integration of Sales Engagement Platform

An e-commerce Indian company has integrated the sales engagement platform, SalesLoft, with its existing CRM, HubSpot. Under this integration, the sales team shall be able to view information on customers right inside SalesLoft, through which the system may communicate individually and track engaging metrics. The integration process involves the definition of fields to be synced and the creation of API connections, then rigorous testing. When integrated and live, the system provides real-time customer interaction insights to the sales team for better engagement with prospects and effectively closing deals.

Training Your Team to Leverage New Technologies Effectively

Introducing new sales enablement tools is not enough. For you to really drive value from these technologies, you need to effectively train your team. Proper training will help the sales team understand how to use the tools and increase their benefits.

Why Train?

- **Adoption:** It is critical to drive adoption. Any well-trained team will certainly be willing to accept the new technologies and actually bring them into daily workflows.
- **Efficiency:** The training reduces the learning curve and enables the team to become proficient in using tools.
- **Effectiveness:** Proper training will ensure the team applies the tools effectively in executing their sales goals—how to use features, analyze data, and make informed decisions.
- **Motivation:** Training can be a motivational tool showing the team that the company cares about growing them professionally.

Designing a Training Program

First of all, calculate the training needs of your sales force. See in what areas they need to be supported, and what skills they require in order to do their jobs effectively.

- **Design a Training Plan:** Based on your needs assessment, formulate a detailed training plan including objectives, content, methods of delivery, and time schedule. Make sure the overall sales strategy is aligned with the plan.

- **Choose Training Methods:** Select appropriate training methods based on what the team wants and the nature of the tools. This can be in a form of classroom training, online tutorials, workshops, and hands-on practice sessions.
- **Development of Training Materials:** Come up with well-elaborated, short, simple, clear material that is easy to understand. This may include user manuals, video tutorials, and interactive guides.
- **Conduct Training Sessions:** Impart the training programs in an organized manner. The trainers should be knowledgeable and in a position to give practical insights. Encourage participation and see that questions and doubts are clarified.
- **Provide Ongoing Support:** Training should not be a one-time affair. Provide for follow-up sessions, refresher courses, and access to resources on a continuous basis. Encourage them to come forward and share their experiences and thus learn from each other.
- **Assessment:** Make sure to measure the effectiveness of the training by measuring performance and getting feedback from the team. This information is then used to make improvements and ensure continuous learning.

Example: Training a Sales Team on a New CRM System

For instance, an Indian healthcare company that wants to implement Salesforce as its new CRM system may start with a needs assessment in areas where support is needed by its sales team. A detailed training plan would then be developed, including online tutorials, hands-on workshops, and one-to-one coaching. The training materials include step-by-step guides, video tutorials, and interactive quizzes. The training sessions shall be led by experienced trainers who provide practical insights and foster participation. There is also follow-up support through check-ins, refresher courses, and a help desk. The trainings' effectiveness is gauged with the observation of performance and feedback from the team to incorporate continuous improvement in the program.

Conclusion

Using technology for sales enablement is an important growth strategy to achieve success in today's competitive business environment. This, therefore, will assist you in best reaping the benefits accruable from these technologies by implementing proper evaluation and selection of the right sales enablement tools, ensuring seamless integration into existing CRM and marketing automation systems, and finally providing your team with effective training. Such strategies shall help an organization to enhance its selling processes, engage its customers better, and realize its goals on sales in the Indian context. Embrace technology and support the continuous learning and development of your sales team to help them maintain their edge for sustainable organization growth.

Chapter 9: Program Launch and Ongoing Management

This is the first and foremost necessary step in introducing any new program into an organization; it governs the success and long-term impact. This could be for a new sales enablement tool, training initiative, or any strategic business process. Strategies to kick-start the programs, robust techniques of change management, and ongoing support are extremely necessary for the successful accomplishment and sustainability of the program. In this chapter, we will review some of the strategies for a successful roll-out program, techniques in change management to work around resistance, and gain insight into the offering of ongoing support and resources for continued success.

Effective Strategies for Program Rollout and Adoption

A new program rollout needs to have proper planning and organization ensuring the program be embraced well, adopted quickly, and used correctly to its potential by all the concerned parties.

Preparations for Launch

Define the Objectives Clearly

Well-defined and measurable objectives can thus be prepared before any program is launched. This does not tie the program to the objectives of an organization but also gives a clear road map to the success of the program.

Engage Stakeholders Early

Engage key stakeholders early in the process so that they may invest in and support it. Such stakeholders would typically include executives, managers, and end-users. Meetings, workshops, and presentations should be organized to share information about the program benefits and to obtain input. For example, in SaaS organization, involving team leaders during the planning phase could help to tailor the program according to the needs of the different teams.

Plan a Detailed Rollout

A detailed rollout plan will present steps, a timeline, and resources needed for the program launch. Such a plan has to include milestones, key activities, and responsibilities. For example, a plan for launching a new CRM system would have phases like pilot testing, user training, and full-scale deployment.

Pilot Program

Conducting a pilot program allows the new initiative to be rolled out on a small scale before full deployment. This testing identifies potential problems and enables feedback in order to fine-tune it. For example, in a healthcare organization, one department would pilot a new patient management system before implementing the system throughout the entire organization.

Implementation Strategies

Communicate Effectively

Effective communication should take place at the launch of the program. Have a communication plan where you will have emails, newsletters, webinars, and face-to-face meetings. Be very clear on the purpose of the program, benefits, and implications on daily operations. Utilize multiple channels to reach all stakeholders with consistent messages.

Complete Training of the members

Successful adoption depends on training. Design apt training modules for the sets of users indicated above. Apply a range of training methods, for example, online modules or workshops, and one-on-one coaching. For example, a financial services firm intended to introduce a new risk management tool. Give analysts, managers, and executives separate sessions.

Providing strong support on the period of transition helps the user to understand the new software. This may include setting up a help desk, access to FAQs and guides on troubleshooting, and appointment of champions in every department that can help peer support. There could also be regular check-ins and feedback sessions that can resolve concerns promptly .

Monitor and Measure Adoption

Track adoption rates to address how well the program is being received. What measurements to consider: usage rate, user feedback, performance improvement.

Example: Rollout of a Program in a Start-up

It begins with involving the team members in the planning phase to gather their input on how the platform could be tailored according to their needs. There is also a detailed rollout plan, including pilot testing in some select departments. Comprehensive training is provided through workshops and online tutorials for all team members. There is effective communication in respect of understanding by all parties regarding the benefits accruing from the usage of and how to use the platform. A support team is in place to assist with any challenges that may arise during the transition. The company has a pulse on adoption through usage analytics and

feedback surveys and makes any necessary adjustment to ensure
success.

Change Management Techniques to Overcome Resistance

Most of the time, the introduction of any kind of change is met
with some amount of resistance, and successful management of this
very resistance determines how smooth the implementation of any
new program would be. Managing effective change means
identifying sources of resistance and using strategies to overcome
them.

Resistance understood

The reasons for resistance to change may be based on fear of the
unknown, lack of trust, perceived negative impacts, and disruption
of established routines. Such sources can be identified and specific
strategies developed to deal with them.

Open Communication

The need is to create trust and adopt transparent communication that limits uncertainty. Explain the need for change, what benefit an individual might gain from the change and how individuals might be affected by the change. Limit anxiety and concern by responding to their fears and anxieties and provide updates on a regular basis during the implementation phase.

Involve Employees in the Change Process

Engaging employees in the process of change enhances their sense of ownership and lessens friction. Seek their views, engage them in the planning, and put up their suggestions in the implementation.

Offer Support and Resources

Providing sufficient support and resources makes adaptation easier for employees. They may include training, information availability, and a support network. Ensure that the employee knows where to turn for assistance, and that issues brought up are given due regard.

Recognize and Reward Adaptation

Positive reinforcement through public recognition, bonuses, and career growth opportunities to those employees who would embrace the change, which then would act as an example to others, can be provided. This reinforces the positive in the change by celebrating small wins.

Address Emotional and Psychological Impact

One of the significant impacts that change may have is on the emotional and psychological fronts. Provide support in the form of counseling, stress management resources, and open forums for discussion. Empathize with the concerns expressed by employees and offer reassurance.

Example: Change Management in a Marketing Company

A marketing company is implementing a new digital documentation system. There is some resistance from employees used to doing things on paper. In managing this change, the company communicates clearly about the gains to be made from working with a digital system, such as efficiency and saving of time from paperwork. The staff are involved at the initiation stage of change management, and their suggestions were considered in the design of the system. Ensures smooth adoption by providing complete training and follow-up support. Recognizes and rewards employees who pick up and start using the new system quickly. Provides counseling and stress management facilities to enable the staff to adjust to the new set-up.

Provide Ongoing Support and Resources for Continued Success

The successful program launch is only part of it. To sustain that success, support and resources will need to be provided well into the future. This maintains momentum, resolves any new issues that may arise, and provides for the ongoing improvement of the program.

Providing an Ongoing Support Structure

- **Helpdesk and Support Team:** Offer a help desk and support team who can assist users out of any trouble they may encounter. The support team should be knowledgeable, responsive, and easily reachable by phone, email, or chat.
- **Knowledge Base and FAQs**: There should be an in-depth knowledge base and an FAQ section to refer to by users for self-support. These will have step-by-step guides related to the usage of the product, troubleshooting, and many other frequently asked questions.
- **Regular Updates and Enhancements:** The program should be continued to be updated and enhanced in keeping with the user feedback and evolving needs. Regular updates of the program keep it relevant and address the problems that might have crept up.

Continuous Training and Development

- **Refresher Courses:** Run periodic refresher courses to update the users in respect of any changes or new features added. It would help to keep up proficiency and further ensure that users get full use out of the program.
- **Advanced Training Sessions:** Advanced training sessions would enable users to enhance their knowledge and skills. It may further consist of specialized workshops, webinars, and certification programs.
- **Peer-to-Peer Learning and Support Groups:** Ensure peer-to-peer learning and support through the implementation of forums, discussion groups, and mentorship programs. To this end, users can be allowed to share their experiences, learn from one another, and build a supportive community.

Monitoring and Evaluation

- **Performance Metrics:** Continuously track the performance of the program by relevant metrics. It could include usage rates, user satisfaction, and impact on business outcomes. These metrics should be reviewed regularly for any improvements.
- **User Feedback:** Take feedback from users in the form of surveys, focus groups, and feedback forms. Based on the

feedback, act on it and make necessary adjustments and enhancements.

- **Regular Reviews and Audits:** The program should be subjected to regular reviews and audits to ensure that it is certain of meeting its objectives, leading to desired outcomes. This helps to pinpoint gaps and areas of improvement.

Example: Continuous Assistance in a Telecommunications Company

Consider a telecommunications company in India that has implemented a new customer relationship management system (CRM). The business sets up a dedicated helpdesk and a supporting team that is available over the phone, e-mail, chat, and so on. There will be a complete knowledge base and FAQ for self-help. Regular updates and enhancements shall be done in accordance with user feedback. The company will also provide refresher courses and advanced training sessions for employees. Forums and discussion groups are encouraged to make use of peer learning and support groups. The metrics to be used in measuring the performance of the program include usage rates and customer satisfaction scores. This will be done through regular reviews and audits to ensure that the objectives of the CRM system have been met.

Conclusion

Hitting up a new program in an organization is a very tricky task but one of the most important tasks. Effective roll-out and adoption strategies of the program, robust techniques of management in change, and on-going support are of much importance. The proper planning of the launch, overcoming resistance, and follow-up support and resources can bring about the best opportunity for programs to be long-term in nature, hence a success. Such strategies will help an organization sail through the unique challenges and opportunities lying ahead and assure growth in the attainment of its strategic goals. These practices will help an organization embrace a culture of continuous improvement and innovation, which is the hallmark of success in any competitive environment.

Chapter 10: Measuring and Optimizing for Impact

Defining Key Metrics and KPIs

Sales enablement is all about equipping the sales teams with tools, content, and information to help them sell more effectively. Key metrics and KPI measurement should be defined and tracked across various aspects of sales to ensure desired outcomes for sales enablement efforts. It provides insights into sales operations, highlighting areas for improvement, allowing for the development of strategies that lead to optimal results.

Sales Productivity Metrics

Sales productivity is one of the core focuses of sales enablement, and a number of metrics are important in measuring it. A key metric is time to first deal - the average time taken to close the first deal for any new sales representative. This metric really shows the efficiency of the onboarding and how ready the new hires are to start contributing to the company's revenue.

These classic leading metrics around sales productivity in sales teams are the number of calls, emails, meetings, and demos that a sales representative is making. Keeping track of the said activity enables the sales leadership to learn and acquire an understanding of the level of engagement that their team has, and patterns connected to corresponding successful outcomes. For instance, an increase in demos might lead to a higher conversion rate, signaling this particular activity as impactful.

Another important yardstick to use while measuring the quality of opportunities a sales team pursues would be the opportunity to win ratio. The comparison of the number of opportunities built against the number of wins registered gives the potential to tell how effective the sales process is, and it can show the quality of the leads as well. More ratios will show that a team is working on high-quality opportunities; lesser ratios are a suggestion that the targeting processes need improvement.

Efficiency Metrics about the Sales Process

Equally important is the efficiency of the sales process, measured by metrics such as the lead velocity rate. LVR gauges the month-over-month growth in qualified leads. This measurement really shows if the sales pipeline is growing or not. Thus, a high LVR means an expanding pipeline and will maintain revenue moving up for longer.

Another important metric is the pipeline coverage ratio between the value of opportunities in the sales pipeline and the sales target. A healthy pipeline coverage ratio will ensure that the sales team has adequate opportunity to meet and exceed sales targets, with reduced risk of shortfalls.

Forecast error is a very essential topic for managing expectations and resources. Comparison between forecasted sales and actual sales shall help companies to further sharpen their forecasting methodology along with processes in order to make better predictions and easy decision-making.

Content Effectiveness Metrics

Content is a key ingredient for sales enablement, and the effectiveness of content can actually be measured under a few different metrics. Content accessibility is basically defined by the ease with which the salespeople can find their way around to their content. It can be tracked by metrics like search effectiveness or time spent searching for content. When content is easily accessible, a salesperson can quickly leverage it with an at-hand customer; the sales process becomes that much more efficient and effective. The performance of sales content can also be taken through the engagement metrics related to time on page or click-through rates. They help to understand how effective the content is with the audience and what kind of impact it has on moving the deals down the pipeline. But also invaluable is sales feedback on content, which might come from things like surveys or direct sales rep feedback. In fact, this qualitative input can be converted into a quantitative metric, such as some number of an average rating, in order to determine just how relevant and useful the material provided is.

Training and Development Metrics

Training and development are integral to the success of sales enablement. Metrics, such as the rate at which submitted training programs are completed, optimize a clear view on the engagement level of sales representatives. By and large, high completion rates would indicate that the reps find enough value in the training and commitment to enhancing skills.

Other critical metrics are learning retention, usually measured through post-training appraisals. This simply represents the amount of knowledge retained by salespeople over time; hence, it speaks to the effectiveness of the training programs. Indeed, its effects on conversion rate can be traced directly so that any such effects on sales outcomes can be used by trainers in possibly refining the training-facilitating programs to have maximum impact.

Customer Experience and Revenue-Related Metrics

Customer experience metrics, such as the customer acquisition cost and the customer retention rate, are very important for the evaluation of the efficiency of the entire Sales Enablement program. CAC measures the cost of acquiring a new customer within an organization and is a metric that organizations realize in the efficiency of the sales and marketing branch. Customer retention rate just represents how successful a company is in maintaining long-term relationships with its customer, which is an absolute value for a sustainable business model.

Revenue-related metrics, such as revenue per sales rep, and growth have significant links to the effects sales enablement has on the financial indicators of a company. Revenue per sales rep is a measure of how productive an individual is, and revenue growth is a measure of how well a company scales its sales efforts.

Cross-Functional Collaboration and Market Penetration Metrics

Finally, cross-functional collaboration and market-penetration-related metrics are key and nest with getting a full view of the effectiveness of sales enablement. Marketing and sales alignment and collaboration scores reflect the level of harmony among various departments and their collaboration in acquiring common goals. Market share growth and geographic penetration metrics uncover how effectively a firm grows its presence within the market—it's that simple and an obvious measure of long-term success.

It goes without saying that closely monitoring these measures and KPIs enables businesses to make sure their sales enablement strategies are working toward impacting real results, and in turn, this drives better sales processes and further assures sustainable business growth.

Creating a Feedback Loop

It is important that a feedback loop continually optimizes sales enablement initiatives. However, this process actually begins with feedback from the sales reps at the very front line of daily customer interaction. Their insights are invaluable for their real-time views of what is working and what is not. Involvement of sales representatives through regular feedback sessions—whatever form it may be: surveys, interviews, or informal conversations—may provide insights into the gaps in the enablement process. The feedback may range from the usability of sales tools to the relevance of the training materials and their effectiveness in different sales situations.

Another important component in the feedback loop is bringing back customer insights. Knowing what your customer thinks can provide a big boost to any sales enablement. This can be done through surveys of actual customers, post-sale interviews, or dissecting the interaction with and feedback from customers captured during the sales process. The insights from the customers about how the process could be smoothed out, made less strenuous, or where extra help could come in handy in satisfying customers with their concerns could be useful. If the same questions are coming up again and again from customers, this could be a cue that improved sales content or more training for the sales team is required.

The other part of the feedback loop would be the analysis of the performance metrics and sales data. Organisations should be able to appreciate the depth at which a sales enablement initiative is faring well by looking at data related to conversion rates, time spent on each sales stage, and specific sales campaigns. It is easier for trends to be established and success and potential areas of problems to be highlighted through data-driven analysis. For instance, if one piece of content significantly outperforms others in driving conversions, the intel on that can be applied to model led success in other areas of the sales process.

Harnessed properly, the analytics provided by a sales enablement platform further strengthens this feedback loop. These platforms most often provide granular data related to the use of the enablement tool by sales teams, which content works best, and maybe where weaknesses lie in the enablement process. Regular analysis of such data will help the organisation make data-driven decisions for the continuous improvement of the sales enablement effort. For example, if reports show that certain training modules are completed infrequently or that specific content is rarely used, this will signal where change is needed on the enablement side.

An effective feedback loop ensures sales enablement is responsive and grows as the needs of the sales team and market change. This will occur when organisations continuously look out for feedback from sales reps and customers, study sales data, and exploit platform analytics. The iterative feedback and optimisation process ensures that the sales enablement initiatives remain effective, relevant, and aligned with the strategic goals of the organisation.

Data-driven Optimization

This is an indispensable element of any effective sales enablement strategy. It requires the analysis of improvement areas, the experimentation with numerous practices, and customization that caters to the specific needs of the sales team in the arena of sales enablement. To do so, it first must analyze the data well drawn from different sources: metrics of sales performance, feedback of sales reps, and customer insights. The organization is now able to identify trends and patterns that may not immediately jump out so that they focus on areas that need changes.

For example, the evidence that some sales reps consistently beat every other sales rep over time may be worthy of delving into what the reps are possibly doing differently. This could involve looking at their use of sales enablement tools, the content they rely on, or their approach to customer interactions. This identification of best practice methods is helpful because, if identified, other sales reps and team members can emulate such practices, and the performance level can be raised for the total team. If the data indicates that the sales are slowing through any given stage, a case can be made that more training may be needed or different sales enablement tools will be required so as to quicken the process.

The power of A/B testing to optimize your sales enablement initiatives. By testing different approaches on small groups of sales reps, organizations can know what works best before the strategies are applied to all members of a team. For instance, an organization can test two different scripts for sales and understand what receives more customer interaction or test different kinds of content formats and understand what drives better engagement rates. These test results can then be taken to make changes that can help fine-tune the sales enablement strategy for maximum effectiveness.

On another level, the personalization of this process brings out still another important component with respect to data-driven optimization. Sales rep capabilities differ considerably; a one-size-fits-all solution to sales enablement will not work. Organizations will surely be in a position to provide a uniquely catered sales enablement experience to every rep if data about the individual performance of the sales rep is analyzed. For instance, a rep who is not so strong at closing deals can be provided with more training in negotiation techniques while a rep who is brilliant at customer engagement may be given higher-level tools in order to increase their already great performance. Such a tailored approach not only increases the performance of the sales rep but also boosts his interest and participation in the sales enablement process.

The last piece in this optimization puzzle is continuous improvement. Sales enablement is not a one-time affair. Rather, it is a continuous process that requires periodic reviews for adjustments. This living model would continuously measure the effectiveness of the sales enablement initiatives for making data-driven adjustments, but it would also ensure the sales team is always armed with the best tools, content, and training to win on the job. This cycle entails regular review of performance numbers, listening to feedback, and testing new approaches to keep the sales enablement approach fresh and effective.

Finally, data-driven optimization is one of those approaches that an organization must incorporate to ensure the full effectiveness of sales enablement initiatives. In fact, using data to surface areas of potential improvements, try the approaches, personalize the experience, and continually develop will assist any company in coming up with an impactful sales enablement strategy that will drive results towards the realization of their business vision.

Measuring the ROI and Demonstrating Value

It is essential to calculate ROI for sales enablement initiatives, as this will help to sensitize the stakeholders to the continuance of support and investment requests. Maximizing ROI involves putting the costs of a calculation-informed sales enablement effort or another against the financial benefits of the same. Benefits include increased revenue, reduced time to get through the sales cycle, better win rates, and improved customer satisfaction. To assess such a return properly, one would need a means of tracking the direct and indirect effects of sales enablement on organizational performance.

Some impacts can be directly measured and quantified: An improvement in this sales revenue due to the sales enablement program can be an example. Or, a recently started sales training initiative could be quantified: "Because of this, my win rates increased by 10%.". Other impacts might be an enhancement of customer satisfaction or a greater probability that a more confident, better-qualified team of salespeople will be developed. While these types of impacts are less immediate or obvious, they are quite significant in their own right and help bring about even more success for the organization.

How to Bring the Impact of Sales Enablement Home to Stakeholders. And stakeholders—from executives to sales leaders and other departments—need to realise how beneficial sales enablement is. This message should not just communicate the ROI figures; it should communicate the quantitative impacts that actually show the positive change sales enablement is making in the sales team and, by extension, the rest of the organization. For instance, it can be shown that success stories shared by sales reps helped by enablement efforts reveal where stakeholders can find value in enablement efforts for themselves.

Another major way to show value is to tie sales enablement with general business performance. There should be no question of considering sales enablement as a function alone but as part of the large picture; it is integral to the goals of the organization. Having the metrics on sales enablement align with business objectives assures that the effort taken in sales enablement contributes to the general success derived out of a company.

For example, if the company's goal is to conquer a new market, then all investments in sales enablement intend to ensure that the sales force—parallel to cross-functional departments such as marketing and product development—is well equipped with knowledge, tools, and content to result in success in the new market. Organizations can further justify continued investment in sales-enablement initiatives if they can be shown to support the organization in the realization of strategic objectives. All other aspects of measuring ROI and demonstrating value should be carried out through reporting and communication with stakeholders on an ongoing basis. This includes updates on developments in sales enablement initiatives, key metrics, and insights, including any changes that occurred based on feedback or performance data. Regular communication informs and includes stakeholders, and it helps ensure that sales enablement remains important and relevant to the business.

Essentially, the measurement of ROI on sales enablement programs and communication of value ensures the initiatives receive the relevant support and investments. This forms the basis on which organizations will be able to go ahead and demonstrate the effect of sales enablement and secure their place as critical sales within the company as a function in its entire strategy formation. Organizations are able to show the impact of sales enablement on different business objectives, and thus it is important that with each report, sales enablement will be aligned with the overall company goals.

Chapter 11: Personalization and Customer Focus

Building Detailed Customer Personas

How well do you really understand who your customers are and what they need? Effective personalization understands that the very first step to this understanding comes from detailed customer personas, which serve as almost living representations of your ideal buyers. A buyer persona is not a demographic profile. It is not a real buyer; it's an imaginary character, semi-fictional, based on real data and insights, embodying key traits, behaviors, and characteristics that represent your target customers, including their goals and challenges. This being the case, businesses have to clearly define these personas to put up effective sales and marketing strategies, adjusting to the requirements of diverse customer segments.

Creating detailed buyer personas means a detailed analysis of factors such as customer demographics, psychographics, buying behavior, and pain points. This all starts from data collection across various sources using customer feedback, including customer interviews, surveys, website analytics, and social media insights. This will help one understand deeply what keeps your customers moving, the problems they are trying to solve, and how they make their purchasing decisions. For instance, whether cost trumps quality or whether customer service to one customer segment is more important than price can mean the world of difference in how you target your messaging to that segment.

Upon capturing the data, the information is segmented according to the personas identified. Market segmentation involves a technique whereby an organization divides its target market into digestible sub-groups that are homogenous in nature. This is instrumental because an organization can target and tailor its messages with much precision. For example, various personas can be identified in a business: the "Budget-Conscious Buyer," the "Tech-Savvy Professional," and the "Eco-Friendly Consumer." Each of them represents a different market segment, with sensitivities, messaging, content, and corresponding offers adapted in kind.

The true value of this exercise lies in using these personas to inform the sales and marketing approach. Matching what is critical to each persona with corresponding strategies can help customer experience become more relevant and compelling. For instance, campaigns can be designed for every particular pain point associated with that persona, such as cost-saving tips for the Budget-Conscious Buyer or sustainable practices for the Eco-Friendly Consumer. With such insights, sales teams are then able to make personalised pitches that will really resonate with the customers, thus leading to more customer engagement and conversion rates.

Secondly, granular awareness of personas can help in reviewing product development and customer service strategies. With an understanding of what matters most for all those different customer segments, the business is better placed to target products, services, and support accordingly. An instance would be to provide advanced features for a Tech-Savvy Professional, but if the technology suddenly becomes strange, focus on ease of use. This is because, at the end of the day, detailed customer personas can enable construction of more tailor-made, relevant, and effective sales and marketing strategies that realise customer satisfaction and loyalty.

How to Implement Personalization at Scale?

In the competitive market of today, personalization has become an essential element to stay in the race; the customers want something that seems tailored at every touchpoint. However, successful broad personalization is the byword of tapping into the power of data, which enables scaled customized experiences across an organization in an efficient and relevant manner.

Data is the backbone of personalization. Businesses can collect information about customer interaction, purchase history, browsing behavior, and so on from different sources in order to understand and decipher individual preferences and behaviors. Derived from such insights, companies develop customized content, messaging, and offers that appeal to customers at a personal level. For example, the e-commerce website could apply such data to recommend products relevant to a particular customer's purchase history or active wish list, hence making the shopping experience more relevant and delightful.

Personalizing content, messaging, and offers goes beyond addressing the customer by the first name. It is all about delivering the right message to the right person at the right time. This involves personalization according to the customer's stage within the buyer's journey, their preferences, and their needs. For example, a customer showing a sign of interest in a particular category of products could be sent personalized emails containing those particular items, perhaps with special offers or discounts. Similarly, website content may dynamically change with the user's behavior to always show whatever is most likely to grab their interest.

Technology plays a major role in enabling personalization at scale. Manage and execute personalized campaigns within the normal operation of the CRM systems, marketing automation platforms, and artificial intelligence tools. These technologies streamline the process of delivering personalized content and offers over a wide variety of channels, including email, social media, and websites. For instance, it would segment clients according to their behavior and preferences for them, and so cause personalization; this will then trigger the email campaigns intended for the said personalization to help in the nourishment of leads all through the sales funnel.

One is expected to measure the effectiveness of personalization operations, understand the correctness of these efforts, make proper data-driven adjustments in this area, and trace the key engagement drivers, projecting from metrics such as conversion rates, customer satisfaction, and revenue growth. From these metrics, businesses will be better positioned to identify which personalization strategies work and where there is room for improvement. More than that, most important, it keeps personalization relevant over time, and it drives better customer experiences and business results through continuous monitoring and optimization of personalization efforts.

In short, making personalization a scalable operation is a multi-layered job that goes through strategic planning based on data and technology. By using these insights to drive personalization, curating content and offers that resonate with individual interests, and using technology to manage and automate campaigns, businesses can create real personal experiences at scale. The outcome is deeper connections with customers, more engagement, and, therefore, more loyal and revenue-generating consumers.

Tailoring Outreach for Maximum Impact

In a society that is subjected to numerous advertisements, the importance of a more tailored outreach to meet the needs and preferences of most customers cannot be overemphasized. Customized outreach does not only make business pop in a crowded marketplace but also goes a long way in assisting in the build-up of rapport and trust with customers, hence more solid and longer-lasting relationships. Getting optimum impact through personalized outreach includes having in mind who your customer really is and a great strategy in delivering content, and also seriously considering constant modifications.

The first step in how to properly customize the outreach would be to make the outreach relevant to the needs and interests of the customer. This includes what may motivate the customer, what challenges they may be facing, and, probably best, the ways in which a product or service provided could offer a solution to them. Businesses are thus able to segment the audience and think about outreach campaigns that may connect with different segments of people due to their unique needs, all based on the data and customer personas. For example, a business targeting small businesses and large enterprises may develop different messaging with different content and, in turn, hone into the specific benefits that each of these may appreciate for their unique challenges and goals.

Personalization is key to creating rapport and trust with customers. What personalization in outreach efforts really does is convey that a business cares about what the customer needs and genuinely wants to help them achieve success. The latter can be implemented through personalized email campaigns, targeted ads in social media, or even personalized landing pages that convey customer interests and preferences. For example, a customer who has interacted with content in regard to a certain product line may, in the future, receive follow-up emails about the same product with more information and related offers. This will act to cement more interest and draw them even closer to their buying solution.

Targeted content and offers are thus crucial to ensuring that personalized outreach is as effective as possible. Your objective is to give the prospect meaningful information along with proper incentives that relate directly to their situation. This might be the discount on an item they have been interested in, a product recommendation based on their purchase history, or case studies showing how other customers like them have used your product or service. By delivering content and offers that really cater to the customer's needs, businesses can increase engagement, drive conversions, and ultimately boost sales.

The importance of measuring the effectiveness of personalized outreach lies in constant improvement. Open rates, click-through rates, conversion rates, and customer feedback are key performance indicators through which you will gauge how well all your outreach efforts resonate with your audience. Businesses will see what works properly and what does not, thus enabling them to data-drive changes to their outreach strategy. For example, if any given email campaign does not pull through as intended, businesses can try changing the subject lines, messaging, or offers in the email to see if they increase better results.

This calls for effective personalization of outreach that must, by design, strategically engage the customer, understand what is needed or preferred, build rapport and trust within the personalization process, and deliver the content or offers being sent. By continually measuring and optimizing the outreach efforts, businesses are guaranteed to have their personalized strategies be effective and relevant in the long haul—ultimately resulting in better customer relations and business outcomes.

The Role of Technology in Personalization

The digital age leverages technology to realize personalization at scale and significantly transforms how businesses engage with their customers. From CRM systems and marketing automation platforms to artificial intelligence and machine learning, these tools enable businesses to deliver personalized experiences tailored to the unique needs and preferences of every individual customer. This enables an organization to have a competitive advantage and build long-lasting relationships with customers.

The main pillars of every personalization strategy are CRM and marketing automation platforms. Most importantly, they enable the collection, storage, and analysis of huge volumes of customer data, thereby making it possible to have an overview of every customer's interactions, preferences, and behaviors. Such real-time information assists companies in audience segmentation, automatization of more personalized types of marketing campaigns, and real-time performance measurement. For example, a CRM system can automatically group customers according to their purchasing history and then send relevant offers or content on subjects in which they are interested. These go a step further to send automatic personalized messages on every relevant communication platform, including emails, social media, websites, and more.

AI and machine learning enable predictive personalization in the field. Such technologies analyze large datasets to identify patterns and trends that even the best human analysts might miss in an effort for businesses to remain one step ahead of emerging customer needs and preferences. For example, an AI recommendation engine identifies what it is that a customer ideally needs on a website based on his browsing history and patterns, the previous transactional data, or even the actions of other similar customers. This level of personalization is usually what really caters to the customer's ego and makes one graduate from just being a regular user to being a loyal customer, as they are ever more engaged with products and offers that interest them in a relevant manner.

Now, as technology is being leveraged to deliver personalization, important concerns around privacy and compliance arise. The more personal data businesses collect and process, they have to remain compliant with the General Data Protection Regulation (GDPR) and the California Consumer Protection Act (CCPA). This, in essence, involves becoming transparent in the manner in which data about customers is collected, stored, and used and giving customers control over their personal information. Businesses that do not put data privacy at the top of their priorities are often faced with legal problems and the loss of customer faith in trusting a business with their data; the latter can be very damaging to brand reputation.

In the future, technology-based personalization will continue. Meanwhile, with strides in AI, machine learning, and big data analytics, higher and higher orders of personalization are now being enabled so that businesses can deliver hyper-personalized experiences based on the unique characteristics of individual customers. This is where a piece of real-time, individual-based service can be: AI-driven chatbots through which one can obtain real-time personalized customer service and AR visualization in one's environment to have a better understanding of the product before buying it. As these technologies permeate the very fabric of daily business operations, the ability to deliver personalized experiences will enhance brand value and serve as a competitive advantage in an increasingly competitive market. The other tools, ranging from CRM systems and marketing automation platforms to AI and machine learning, help businesses understand their customers to be able to predict what is pertinent for their customers and offer them relevant content and offers. As technology continues to advance and develop, its rigours make survival in this market challenging, except for the well-equipped.

Chapter 12: Creating a Collaborative Sales Ecosystem

Importance of Cross-Functional Collaboration

A sales ecosystem is a complexly interconnected network of teams, tools, processes, and technologies set in motion to drive growth. This contrasts with older, more conventional sales models, which focus only on the sales department. A sales ecosystem unites crucial organizational functions like marketing, product development, onboarding, and customer success. In this way, it allows much better comprehensive visibility to the things the customer might want and a more coherent strategy around how to deal with those needs.

Cross-functional cooperation in a sales ecosystem has many advantages. It drastically improves the entire customer experience by having all teams united under the identical message and goals that are aligned in marketing, sales, product, onboarding and customer success. This has the potential for making different possible ways to seamlessly answer customers' needs for every one of them. This alignment also translates into increased productivity through the shared resources and better visibility, hence reducing redundant effort and shortening the time taken for a sale. Additionally, cross-functional collaboration drives innovation as it taps into more dimensions of views and perspectives, thereby finding more creative resolutions or solutions to business challenges.

One of the most potent barriers to effective cross-functional collaboration, however, is the presence of siloed teams. Siloed teams are teams where very little to no interaction takes place and no communication is exchanged among the teams. The result will be misaligned goals, clashing priorities, and, in the end, customers receiving a mix of messages—all but an ideal recipe for disastrous customer experience and business performance. On top of these, the information-sharing problem of siloed teams may negatively affect decision-making and further lengthen the sales process.

Developing a collaborative selling ecosystem will mitigate these challenges, for which there should be a transition in mindset from teams working with a "me-first" approach to a "we-first" approach. Breaking these silos and fostering a culture of collaboration can unlock the full potential of the sales ecosystem, driving better customer outcomes and sustained growth.

Align Sales, Marketing, Product, and Customer Success

The key to building a successful sales ecosystem is to align the key competencies: sales, marketing, product development, and customer success. This ensures that each department is speaking together, synching up on goals, with joint efforts being complementary and not duplicative or contradictory.

It all begins simply with alignment across functions and creating a shared vision and goals. A shared vision will direct all the teams clearly and give assurance that all are working for the same end. A vision that is customer-centric and focused on how one best serves customers addresses, their needs, solves problems, enhances life, and helps them fulfill themselves. Then, having determined this vision, it needs to be broken down into precise, measurable objectives which each of the teams has to attain. Thus, these must be aligned across departments to make sure all efforts are directed toward common overall goals.

Alignment would further mean well-defined roles and responsibilities of the teams involved in this sales ecosystem working toward achieving shared goals and driving qualitative leads. For example, marketing could be focused on providing leads, the sales team converting leads to paying customers, the product team delivering solutions that meet customer needs, and the customer success team retaining customers. Clearly defined roles will enable organizations to cut down on overlaps, and each team will then be able to focus on its core competencies.

Effective communication is at the heart of cross-functional collaboration. This coordination can easily slip back into siloes without transparent and open communication. Then, realise the communication channels and collaboration frameworks so that teams can interact regularly and harmoniously. This can be the creation of weekly cross-functional meetings, shared project management tools, or even collaboration platforms that allow for the sharing of real-time information. Additionally, the teams are likely to be more cohesive and make sure the efforts are directed towards solving the problem before it can balloon into a big issue through a no-hold-back, blunt feedback culture.

Leverage technology of the contemporary collaboration tools and platforms; some of the most effective include CRM systems, marketing automation tools, and project management software. These are technologies that bring fluidity in communication, information sharing, and management of tasks which all teams are working on within a single playbook. In addition, data analytics tools are capable of providing insight into customer behavior and preferences in activities to make the teams' choices in support of the shared vision and goals from a database of data.

That's the alignment of sales, marketing, product, and customer success: a frictionless sales ecosystem that keeps customer satisfaction, loyalty, and business growth running smoothly. It'll keep your teams focused on common goals, with role definition clear, communication open, and the right technology backing those efforts.

How Leaders Can Drive Collaboration?

This is a very pivotal role for leadership: governing the collaboration that cuts across functions in a sales ecosystem. Leaders need to set the pace for collaboration; they must set up a culture that appreciates the essence of teamwork and cooperation, whereas all the other groups are kept on a similar wavelength pertaining to their efforts.

The culture of collaboration is generated by leaders, who first model the behaviour to be collaborative. When the leader gets involved with the various working teams, solicits ideas from other departments, and shows that their ideas are important in the decision-making process, it sends a very strong message that is effective and collaborative. This encourages those in teams to reciprocate, which will work to break silos and encourage an integrated approach toward meeting goals.

The other vital role of a leader is to enable the building of trust and respect among teams. Team collaboration can only be successful if the members trust each other and have respect for their expertise and contribution. This can also be developed by leaders through transparency, facilitation of open communication, and recognition and celebration of the achievements of different cross-functional teams. The least that the leader needs to do is to ensure that all the teams within the organization exercise an equal opportunity for inclusion in the process of making decisions. This creates a sense of ownership, responsibility, and the vital aspect of being part of the decision-making process within the organization.

Measure and incentivise this: It is key to sustaining a collaborative culture. Leaders should put in place the kind of metrics that track cross-functional collaboration: the number of joint initiatives, how often they are, the success rate of collaborative projects, and the feedback from team members regarding the weights of the collaboration process. Such metrics are the most important because they shed light on the kind of collaborative effort involved and could, therefore, point out areas that need to be increased. For example, incentive plans, such as bonuses or award recognitions, need to be provided to these teams that highly collaborate on the assigned tasks and accomplish the shared organizational objectives and goals.

Dealing with resistance to change is another great issue in encouraging collaboration. People might be used to working in silos, as well as fearing their dilution in influence and control. Leaders will have to address these concerns by clearly articulating the benefits of collaboration, training, and support to help teams adapt to new ways of working, as well as dealing with deeper issues that may be driving the resistance. Leaders can, therefore, take a proactive approach toward managing change to help teams embrace collaboration and fully participate in the sales ecosystem.

So, conclusively, leadership is a necessity for a successful collaboration ecosystem in sales. Leaders who drive a high level of a culture of collaboration, build trust and respect within teams, measure and drive collaboration, and institute change to overcome resistance will gain superior results from cross-functional collaboration. This, in turn, gains better customer outcomes, higher innovation, and sustained business growth.

Case Studies and Best Practices

Successful collaboration across functions is now a reality and has been proven to create very practical, tangible results in real-world applications. Some of them have already put impactful collaborative sales ecosystems in place that others can learn from valid examples of useful lessons in best practice.

Take, for example, Company A, a technology firm that has managed to align sales, marketing, and products in the realisation of its rapid growth. With such a vision, [Company A] galvanised all the teams to work in concert toward a common direction of leaving the customer satisfied, instituting the meeting structure across functions and enabling everyone with collaboration tools. This is how the sales cycle was shortened by 12%, and customer retention was improved by 15%.

Company B, a consumer goods company, was another good example of cross-functional collaboration for launching a new range of products. From the very early stages of designing a product, the sales, marketing, and product teams jointly worked to incorporate customer feedback into the design. By aligning these efforts, maintaining open lines of communication, and incorporating customer feedback into the design process from the very beginning of the product's development, Company B launched the product in time, and the sales team beat the sales targets by 30% in the first quarter.

In this respect, these case studies outline key takeaways for establishing a collaborative selling ecosystem: one alignment around a common vision and goals. Without it, teams are misaligned, which results in resources being wasted and opportunities being missed. The second is communication for successful collaboration. The tool should be accessible to all, meetings should be frequent, and feedback should be open. Leadership is thus key in promoting a culture of collaboration. Leaders need to exhibit endorsements, inculcate trust among the teams and resources and provide support to maintain the process of collaboration.

Future trends are more about intensive data analytics, AI as a tool in making decisions and adopting an agile methodology to bring the team's focus toward driving more collaboration across functions in any sales ecosystem. These trends will continue to develop opportunities in a way that allows adaptable companies to meet the changing market conditions and causes cross-functional collaboration in support of customer needs for the realisation of long-term success.

In summary, sales development calls for deliberate collaboration, heightened leadership, and continuous improvement of the collaboration function, among other factors. With learning from the winning cases described and through monitoring trends to be aware of what could disrupt, organizations will be in a far better position to deploy a sales ecosystem that doesn't stop at accomplishing but rather over-achieves objectives for customer satisfaction, innovation, and growth.

Chapter 13: Data-Driven Sales Enablement

Sales enablement has seen a massive evolution in the last couple of years with the growing availability of data and advanced analytics tools. Data-driven sales enablement involves the strategic employment of data to inform and optimize the sales process, right from understanding customer needs to refining sales strategies and tactics. And use the power of the data to probe deeper into sales operations, personalize content, and, therefore, improve sales results. This chapter will dwell on a discussion about how data can actually transform the process of sales enablement, the use of predictive analytics and artificial intelligence, and effectively leveraging data to create a more impactful but personalized sales process.

Harnessing Data And Insights To Drive Improvement

The amount of data associated with the digital era is colossal; it gives sales teams food for thought toward better decision-making. However, the most important thing is not the volume of this data but the capacity to mine actionable insights from it. Data-driven sales enablement starts from collecting and analyzing relevant data, which, from all indications, presents a foundation for making informed decisions to drive sales performance.

One of the principal benefits of being data-guided is an integrated view of the sales process. These teams can trace every single activity from the outlook at the point of the generation of the lead to the final deal, hinting at better recognition than the patterns and trends. For example, with a win-loss analysis, it is easier for organizations to comprehend the differences between the winning behavior and the one that caused the failure. This kind of data could bring to light important issues, such as the efficacy of the sales messaging, the timing for follow-up, and the characteristics of the top-converting leads. Armed with those sorts of data, sales teams can focus their strategies on the best opportunities moving forward while avoiding a few common pitfalls.

Data-driven sales enablement also implies the possibility for constant improvement. Traditional sales methods often base themselves on intuition or experience, which is very valuable but not a subjective premise by a bias-generating process. Objective, evidence-based, reliable, and scalable approaches are possible. By regularly analyzing sales data, companies are able to identify areas where performance is lagging and can course-correct. That usually means training program restructuring, sales optimizations, or reallocating resources to these high-potential areas.

Making Data Personal and Increasing Scale

Personalization is indeed now a buzzword in sales and marketing, maybe more than a trend. Today, with more and more tight competitive landscapes, the experiences have to be tailor-made directly toward their challenges and needs. Data is behind this type of personalization, allowing sales teams to deliver the right content to their prospects at the right time.

In simple terms, sales enablement personalization involves getting up close and personal with prospects by understanding their unique characteristics and preferences. In the entire data, enough hearsay comes from customer engagement, browsing behavior analysis, activity on social media, or even purchase history. When that data is analyzed, it helps the customers to understand what they need, the challenges they face, and how they prefer to engage with representatives.

Based on this information, sales teams can work to develop hyper-personalized content that is relevant to every prospective customer. For example, if data indicates that a certain prospect is interested in a given feature, the sales team will find a way of emphasizing it during the sales process. Data is not only personalized to bring out sales content but can also be used in sales interactions with timing.

Data-driven personalization doesn't happen at the interaction level but at the level of the entire journey taken through sales. By mapping the buyer's journey and deriving insights into data at each of the different stages, sales teams can point out opportunities to personalize content and engagement strategies. For example, it may be revealed that early-journey prospects respond to educational content, whereas those farther along should be supplied with in-depth product comparison information. By aligning with the buyer's journey, the content strategy of a sales team helps make the sales funnel easier to define, which ultimately shows it has the potential to increase conversion rates.

Exploring Predictive Analytics and Artificial Intelligence Applications within Sales Enablement

Perhaps the most thrilling aspects of data-driven sales enablement include predictive analytics and artificial intelligence. These technologies will empower any sales team to stop being reactive and start proactively engaging in efforts that allow them to predict customer needs and discover new opportunities even before they arise.

Predictive analytics basically involves utilizing past data to forecast potential future results. Sales enablement could be applied to a number of things. Perhaps the most common application of predictive analytics in the lead management process is in the field of predictive models that score the probability of a lead converting into a customer. From past lead data, such as demographic information, behavioral patterns, and history of engagement, predictive analytics would lead to a score that would reflect the probability of conversion. This helps salespeople concentrate on high-potential leads; hence, they are more effective and stand a greater chance of success.

Another very strong application of predictive analytics is sales performance forecasting. Traditionally, the sales function area is judged through rudimentary forecast systems that are either gut-based or a very primitive extrapolation from past performance, both of which are, understandably, very rarely reliable. Predictive analysis, in contrast, uses advanced algorithms to analyze many variables, including market trends and individual sales rep performance, to come up with a more precise forecast in relation to real cash returns. Such forecasts can be very helpful to a sales leader; they can really optimize resource allocation, target setting, and strategy development.

AI takes predictive analytics just an inch further by affording smartness and automation on it. AI-driven technological apparatus is able to read enormous datasets in real-time, identify patterns, and make recommendations that many times would be impossible for human beings to see. For instance, it has the capability to study a prospect's general reaction to a company's website, social media channels, and email campaigns—all in the expectancy of a final purchase from the digital footprints they leave. Based on that, the AI system will prescribe to the sales rep the next best action, whether to send some particular piece of content, schedule a meeting, or make a direct offer.

AI can also be harnessed to automate routine tasks, thus freeing sales reps to engage more in strategic activities. For instance, in clarifying initial queries and qualifying leads for appointments, AI serviced by chatbots can do all of the above rather seamlessly, without any human intervention. This will not only make the system efficient, but it will also care for the prospects by giving them timely and correct responses, hence improving their general experience.

One of the gems in the many exciting prospects of AI in the arena of sales enablement is the possibility of hyper-personalization. If data-driven personalization was all about analyzing past interactions and behaviors, AI could make that step forward in personalization by making content adaptive and altering the strategies in real time. For instance, an AI system might be able to analyze the responses of a given prospect on a sales call and, in real time, suggest differential talking points or content that would align with what they are interested in. The impact of such responsiveness on the effectiveness of sales interactions is profound, with improvements in conversion and stronger customer relationships.

However, the push toward predictive analytics and AI in sales enablement also comes with some challenges. First and foremost, data quality is often a concern. This is because predictive models and AI stand only on data fed to them: they could be very advanced models, but their insights would be very poor, leading to wrong decision-making if the data are of low quality. It follows that organizations have to invest in data management practices that ensure the accuracy and dependability of data. This is precisely the reason for bringing out the concept of continuous data cleaning, validation, and enrichment so as to have state-of-the-art databases.

Adding predictive analytics and AI directly to legacy sales processes and systems is hard to integrate. New technologies, especially ones that are poised to change the foundations of sales, are not easily welcomed by the sales teams. As such, organizations must provide the correct training and support to their sales reps, empowering them to understand the value and utility of these tools in such a way that predictive analytics and AI systems engage the CRMs and other sales platforms seamlessly in order to transition naturally with as little disturbance as possible.

The Future of Data-Driven Sales Enablement

Data will increasingly become central to enabling sales. Companies that are able to take advantage of being data-driven in their strategies are thus best prepared in order to compete in the market. As more and more data turns into insights and improvement, the top elements that will shape a successful sales operation will involve personalized content, predictive analytics, and artificial intelligence.

It's not the data-driven sales enablement technology but the data culture in which everything in the sales process is enveloped. This demands a continuous learning commitment and adaptability to the investment in tools and resources underpinning the operationalization of data strategies.

As we move forward, however, data will continue to play a larger part in sales enablement. Analyses will grow even sharper with enhancements to artificial intelligence and machine learning, which begin to provide an even higher level of automation, in turn allowing sales teams to rapidly hone in on customer needs and tailor those engagements. All the while, technology is increasing, and sales enablement increases to be more predictive, helping organizations stay ahead of the competition continuously while meeting the never-static demands of the customer.

In other words, deriving data insights and personalizing content and sales strategies would drive optimization at a higher scale of efficiency, effectiveness, and customer satisfaction. With every innovation and development in tools and techniques for data-driven sales enablement, companies and people who embrace these changes will be well-positioned to lead industries and excel in the long term.

Chapter 14: Scaling Your Sales Enablement Efforts

A sales enablement effort must be accomplished as a business continues to burgeon and mature. What might be efficacious for a small squad or a startup could be insufficient for larger, more cerebrally confident organizations. Scaling sales enablement is the process of not only amplifying the strategies in place but also preparing for an important next step that includes adapting to new challenges, managing organizational change, and adopting new emerging technologies like artificial intelligence and machine learning. This chapter will look at how to do that effectively and really deal with the challenges that come with organizational growth by embracing state-of-the-art technologies.

Benefits Of Growing Sales Enablement As A Function

Sales enablement would be a superpower-arming your sales team with the right weaponry of tools, content, and information to bring in more deals. Just imagine a cricketer going onto the field with the best bat, the perfect technique, and a solid game plan. That's what sales enablement does for your sales team.

This nurtures productivity. With your sales representatives having easier and faster access to relevant content and training, they can reduce time searching for information and more time selling. It's like having a well-organized toolkit-everything is at their fingertips, and they can focus on what they do best: build relationships and close deals.

Second, sales enablement enhances customer experience. When the salespeople are better equipped, they can present more personalized and relevant solutions to their customers. This engenders trust and builds better relationships-relationships founded upon a very solid foundation for long-lasting success. Just think about going into a store and the salesperson immediately grasping your needs, introducing you to exactly what you would want. That's the kind of experience sales enablement helps create.

Finally, it better aligns the sales and marketing teams. With a good sales enablement strategy, both teams work in harmony. Marketing is preparing the content needed by sales, while sales are providing the feedback that helps marketing fine-tune their strategies. This makes sure that everybody is in sync, working toward one common goal, and driving effective results for the business.

In other words, sales enablement is the secret sauce that makes your sales team better, your customers happier, and your business more successful. The bottom line is that everyone wins.

How to Scale Your Program as Your Business Grows?

Scaling a sales enablement program is much more than simply doing more of the same. It requires a strategic approach that takes into account increasing problems in growing businesses, the need for consistent execution across larger teams, and the requirement to maintain or even improve your efforts. Among the first challenges you'll face when growing your business is how to scale your sales enablement strategies. The things working for a small firm, such as personalized training sessions or one-on-one coaching, become impractical as your selling force grows. Therefore, the initial step in scaling will be standardizing processes and creating reusable systems that can be applied throughout the organization.

This calls for an elaborate and fully executed sales enablement framework that has complete documentation of processes, standard training modules, and tools that are automated. This should be flexible in the face of diverse requirements raised by several sales teams in managing continuity in messaging and methods. For instance, don't make every single asset totally customized to each separate rep; build a library of content, including a mix of resources for various sales scenarios, industries, and buyer personas. This means a sales representative will have easy access to exactly what they need and when it is needed, without ongoing involvement from the sales enablement team.

As organizations scale, the opportunity for effective communication and collaboration among departments further expands. Sales enablement should move from merely a selling function in support of the sales team to a collaborator with marketing, product development, customer success, and other units. This kind of cross-functional alignment is essential to ensure that the sales team is armed with current information, messages, and tools. It talks about the regular cadence of communications between Sales Enablement and other departments: joint planning, shared dashboards, and embedded feedback loops for continuous improvement. A key to cultural collaboration, it will ensure that everything you do with sales enablement knits into the larger business strategy to ensure the best, cohesive, and effective outcomes.

Other key ingredients to scaling include leveraging technology for rationalization and automation of the sales enablement process. As your sales team scales, manual activities start to become very cumbersome and consume the time that could have been better utilized. Automation tools help handle the routine tasks of enabling sales, such as how the content is distributed, how its administration and training will be done, and its performance tracking. For instance, an LMS can automate module delivery, monitor progress and offer customized learning paths based on individual needs. Similarly, a CRM integrated with sales enablement tools can serve the content in an automated manner for a sales representative at the correct time in the sales process, thereby eliminating huge manual efforts in content curation.

Scaling sales enablement means more than simply putting in place the right armoury of tools and associated processes; it means giving the team a new set of skills and resources to survive and thrive in a wider and more complex selling environment. This sometimes takes investments in new training resources, new hiring, or operational restructuring within the sales enablement function to better serve organizational needs. For example, scaling your business might mean you need to start specializing roles within the sales enablement team, such as content strategists, data analysts, or training specialists, so the workload and added complexity become manageable.

Managing Organizational Changes and New Team Dynamics

Growth inevitably brings change and new challenges in managing organizational dynamics. As sales teams grow in size, the ability to maintain a cohesive culture and execution becomes more challenging. The addition of team members, new leaders, and departments can disrupt already optimized processes. This requires managing changes second by second and sustaining a culture of continuous improvement to scale enablement throughout the organization.

Probably one of the biggest challenges with change in an organization is alignment with the sales team. New members may bring different experiences, expectations, and working styles that make the general alignment of sales strategies inconsistent. To be able to address this, it is paramount to create a very robust onboarding program which would not only train the new recruits about the products dealing and the sales processes but also inculcate within them the culture and values of the organization. This includes an onboarding process that is well connected with the enablement of sales to ensure that all new recruits get the same message and are equipped with tools and all resources for success.

Besides onboarding, what also remains crucial to deal with the new team dynamics is the continuous process of training and development. Eventually, as your sales force grows, that group of people is likely to become more diversified, both in terms of skill level and experience in your sales representative role. Some of them may be seasoned professionals who will need some advanced training, while others may be rather freshmen in sales and could be looking for more basic support. There is little likelihood of success with a one-size-fits-all approach to training in this context. For example, a tiered training program with different levels of content can be considered. This allows more targeted and relevant training to be offered, thereby impacting performance more generally and accelerating the onboarding process.

Leadership alignment is another key factor in the organizational change management process for the sales enablement initiative. Anytime there are new leaders or managers, they very likely have new ideas regarding sales approaches or even priorities. Engaging these leaders early on and getting them involved in the planning and execution of the sales enablement strategies can play a key role in building buy-in and ensuring that the entire leadership team is aligned around the direction of the sales enablement program. More practically, regular communications and feedback loops between the sales enablement function and leadership can mitigate issues or misalignments well before issues arise or grow into big problems.

The makeup of the sales enablement team itself may also shift as an organization expands. In smaller companies, sales enablement is often a one-man band or small team that wears many hats. The need for more specialized roles within the sales enablement team will arise as the organization scales. Perhaps at that time, it will include a content strategist dedicated to the development and distribution of sales materials, a training specialist responsible for the design and delivery of the ongoing education program, and a data analyst to track and report on performance metrics. With these roles in place, you'll know that every area of sales enablement receives specialized focus from an expert on how to best serve the sales team.

Change management also highlights the need to be responsive to changes in the requirements of the sales team. When the sales reps mature within the organization, they might feel equipped to deal with another set of challenges—entering new markets, selling more complex products, or moving into new geographies where the competitive environment is different. The sales enablement team must be agile, therefore, able to adapt quickly to such shifting dynamics, helping sales reps overcome those changes with the right support and resources. This might involve developing new content, revising training programs, or implementing new tools and technologies to better support the sales team.

Summing it up

As Sarah learned through the various Sales enablement strategies and began implementing them in her business, she saw drastic changes. Not only did her business flourish, but she also was in a position to measure the changes and understand her consumers better. These techniques not only helped her in profitability but also built consistency and a brand reputation. With Sarah, there was definitely a learning curve, with several ups and downs. But she understood that becoming better takes time and patience. Now, with her newly acquired knowledge on sales enablement strategies, she is ready to take over the market.

Effective scaling your sales enablement operation as your business grows is complex yet necessary. It demands a strategic touch with consideration and alignment about the needs of standard processes, cross-functionality, and effective utilization of technology. Managing organizational changes and new team dynamics are equally important, along with the adoption of emerging technologies like AI and machine learning. It is by addressing these and taking advantage of the new tools at your disposal that you will be better able to scale enablement and help the organization in its continued success.

Key Takeaways:

- Sales enablement a strategic method in which training, content, and technology all come together to empower the sales force.
- It is important to understand the subtlety of selling in a B2B versus a B2C market. Each market varies, and sales enablement allows you to tailor your approach to fit the needs of whom you serve.
- Success in sales enablement rests on a solid foundation-through well-defined processes, robust training programs, and the right technological tools-to give your team the needed preparation for any kind of sale.
- In the modern sales environment, data is king. The use of data can enhance sales outcomes and can turn customer relations from being just sales to effective, customer-responsive sales efforts by personalizing it.
- As your business scales, so should your sales enablement. Scaling effectively means adapting to the change in organizations, embracing new technologies like AI and machine learning, and ensuring your sales strategies evolve with your business.

Imagine being the cricket coach, where one knows full well their team has the winning potential but, without those abilities being tapped into, trained upon, and strategized, they remain second-best.

Similarly, sales enablement can help give that secret sauce serving to your selling team; it means going from zero to high-performing, led by a squad of well-oiled sales representatives and not an idea.

It's a lot more than giving your team some extra training or better technology. Sales enablement is essentially all about closely aligning the efforts of your sales team with the bigger objectives of your business. Whether you are a B2B or a B2C enterprise, the first step in knowing how to approach the market and build strategies accordingly is by understanding it. It's there that sales enablement does its mojo: to lead you through the maze of your market and keep your sales teams prepared, informed, and armed for closing.

Ready to finally take your sales team to the next level? Let's begin by implementing all that you learnt in this book!

Verses Kindler Publication

Reach us through our website -
https://www.verseskindlerpublication.com/
For more information visit our Instagram or Facebook page.

* 9 7 8 9 3 5 6 0 5 4 3 1 8 *